A SWING
FOR LIFE

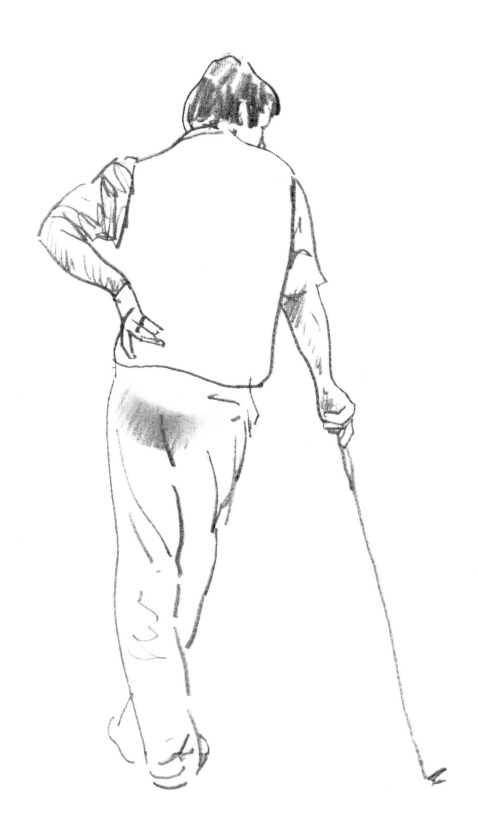

A SWING FOR LIFE

Nick Faldo

with Richard Simmons

PHOTOGRAPHY BY DAVID CANNON
ILLUSTRATIONS BY HAROLD RILEY

A CHAPMANS BOOK

WEIDENFELD
& NICOLSON

To Gill and the family,
my friends
and Team Faldo

A Chapmans Book
First published in Great Britain in 1995 by
Weidenfeld & Nicolson

The Orion Publishing Group Ltd
Orion House,
5 Upper Saint Martin's Lane,
London, WC2H 9EA

A catalogue reference is available from the British Library

ISBN 0 297 81562 8

Designed by Robert Updegraff
Typeset by Deltatype Ltd, Ellesmere Port, Cheshire
Printed in Italy

CONTENTS

Introduction

I first took an interest in golf in 1971. Charles Coody won the Masters that year, with Johnny Miller and Jack Nicklaus tied for second. I caught a glimpse of the final round on television. Enough to make me curious. It was the Easter school holiday, and I booked a series of six lessons at a local club, Welwyn Garden City.

Naturally, I expected to be out on the course beating balls in no time. The assistant pro, Chris Arnold, had other plans. He laid down the rules and set about teaching me the basics of grip and 'stance', as it was known then. In fact, as I remember it, he didn't let me loose on a ball until our third meeting.

Still, I was bitten hard. Cycling and swimming had been my only real interests – I was no scholar – and now golf was about to take over. I fell in love with the challenge, and as my ambition proved genuine my parents bought me a half-set of clubs for my fourteenth birthday. I was off and running.

My journey through the junior ranks was a fairly typical one. I was fortunate enough to become a member at Welwyn, and the head professional at that time, Ian Connelly, took me under his wing. It was the start of a relationship that would span more than ten years. Ian was a wonderful coach, and my enthusiasm for the game was only matched by his own. He convinced me that I had the potential to make a name for myself on the amateur scene, and went out of his way to help me work on my swing. During the summers I would split my time between the course, the practice ground and the putting green. I would putt for hours. Like most golf-crazed youngsters, I was soon in possession of a lethal short game, and my handicap tumbled into single figures.

Ian was particularly motivated by the importance of getting the 'simple' things right from the start – the grip, the set-up and so on – and that attention to such fundamental detail has been a feature of my game ever since. He also taught me the meaning of 'rhythm', and my ability to swing every club in the bag at a comfortable pace could still be my greatest asset. Chapter 4 is devoted entirely to the matter of tempo and timing, the introduction to which takes me back to those days as a junior. The practice ground at Welwyn was barely 150 yards long, and I remember standing there with a 3-iron in my hands while Ian challenged me to hit shots with a full swing that landed *short* of the boundary fence.

'The easier you swing, the better you'll hit it,' he used to say. And of course he was right. By the time I left school at the age of 16 I had set my mind on becoming a pro, and told my teachers as much. 'Only one in a thousand ever makes it,' one said, which only made me more determined.

As a tall and willowy teenager, my swing was always prone to being fairly upright. I don't suppose I helped matters by trying to copy the likes of Nicklaus and Johnny Miller – players who at that time believed very much in working the club away from the ball with a deliberately wide one-piece takeaway. But that was the fashion. Teaching at that time also tended to focus on the role of the hands and legs, and was littered with clichés: 'Drive your legs for power', we were told; 'reach for the sky and watch it fly'. Like so many young players of that generation, I ended up with the characteristic reverse-C follow through. With so much independent movement going on, the success of my swing rested entirely on the quality of my hand action through impact. 'Feel' was everything.

To cut a long story short, I had a great hand action but a lousy body movement. These elements of my swing were at odds when they should have been working together. I had to practise hard every day just to maintain a consistent level of ball-striking, though of course my rhythm helped tremendously. And I was lucky. If my timing was ever slightly off, my short game usually got me out of jail.

In 1975 it all clicked beautifully, and I had my best ever season as an amateur. I won a record ten events, including the Berkshire Trophy, the English Amateur and the British Youths' Championship. I turned pro the following season and worked with Ian on and off for a further seven years after that. We continued to be a successful team. He inspired me to a Ryder Cup debut in 1977, and the following year I won my first big professional tournament, the Colgate PGA Championship.

It has changed somewhat now, but in those days America was regarded as the real testing ground, and I was drawn to it. My ambition all along was to win a major championship, and to do that I had to first prove myself capable of competing at the highest level. And so, in 1981, I went to play full-time on the US Tour, which was quite a shock. I had established myself as one of the top players in Europe, but rubbing shoulders day-to-day with the likes of Tom Watson and Jack Nicklaus opened my eyes to a whole new game. These were the best players in the world, and they struck the ball like the best players in the world.

What I noticed most of all was that the players who were winning regularly seemed to be able to shape their shots so much more consistently then I ever could. A steep angle of attack (the inevitable consequence of driving too hard with the legs) caused me to hit the ball with a volatile 'ballooning' trajectory, and so my game was vulnerable in any kind of wind.

The turning point came early in 1983. After closing with two rather lacklustre rounds of 76-76 in the Masters, I decided to spend a week working on my swing down in Texas. Out on the range one day I met the American Ryder Cup player, Mark O'Meara, and he watched me play. As I hit balls, Mark noticed that I was 'lagging' the clubhead behind my hands during the takeaway, and that this caused my backswing to be much too steep. He went on to say that I should work on 'fanning' the clubface open as I moved it away from the ball. Apparently it was something Ben Hogan had suggested he try. Little did I know then the extent to which this innocent advice would affect my career.

I stayed out on the range for three days solid until I felt comfortable with what was at that time a radical move. It certainly made a difference. 'Fanning' the clubface made me rotate my left forearm away from the ball, and that in turn encouraged my arms to swing more around my body. It gave me a flatter and more powerful plane. I started to hit the ball lower, with a more determined, penetrating trajectory. For a brief spell I felt very comfortable with my new-found swing and my confidence was high. On my return to Europe I won four tournaments in the space of six weeks.

But, as you expect of the one-line fix, the effects gradually wore off, and during the 1983 Open Championship at Birkdale I came crashing back to earth. I had a taste of the lead with nine holes to play in the final round, and the pressure hit me like a runaway train. A sharp short game had helped to put me in contention, but when the crunch came I was out of my depth. While Tom Watson fired his shots at the flag on his way to a fifth Open title, I lost the thread and eventually washed up in a tie for eighth place.

I first met David Leadbetter at Sun City the following year. He watched me on the practice tee and gave me one or two ideas to work on. His knowledge and enthusiasm for his subject were overwhelming. He talked about the mechanics of the swing in a language that I had never heard before, and I was taken with his style.

David told me what I already knew: to achieve my goal of winning a major championship I had to work on eliminating the inconsistencies in my method and develop a swing that would repeat under pressure. But he also talked about things I didn't know. Emphasizing the role of the bigger muscles in the body for control, David explained that I needed to stabilize my swing with a passive leg action and, in so doing, create a 'resistance' to the rotation of my trunk. Like winding a spring, I should learn to coil my upper body over the resistance of my knees and hips to create 'torque' – energy I could then release to drive my downswing through the ball. In what he described as a truly 'athletic' motion, the arms would be encouraged to swing in harmony with the movement of the body, while the hands essentially would remain passive throughout.

What impressed me most about David Leadbetter was the depth of his knowledge. To every question he had a logical answer, and that only made me inquisitive to find out more and more. I didn't just want to *fix* my swing, I wanted to *understand* my swing. Six months after that first meeting, I invited David to 'throw the book at me'. At 28 years of age, I was back in school, and every aspect of my game was under scrutiny.

We started with the basics. David taught me to think in terms of creating a more athletic posture at address – a set-up position that pre-determines a good body turn, or 'pivot'. I learned how to control my swing with the rotation of the bigger and more dependable muscles in the torso, and to synchronize the movement of my arms and the club accordingly.

'The dog wags the tail' is how David likes to sum up his philosophy, and it's a principle of control that I have found applies as readily to the short game and putting as it does to the full swing.

It was no overnight success. The transformation took time and hard work. But gradually, as I eliminated superfluous motion and learned to trust the role of my body, I developed a much more compact, repeating swing. The exaggerated leg-slide that once had caused me so many problems was replaced with a more supportive lower body action, while the reverse-C that typified the 1970s made way for the more rounded follow-through position that you see today.

Above all, as a result of the changes we made, my new swing gave me a flatter and more powerful angle of attack and, as a result, my ball-striking improved. I found that I was able to produce a consistent flight pattern with every club in the bag. For the first time in my career I felt that I had real control of the ball and, better still, I understood *why*.

So how does this potted biography help your game?

It's quite simple. I have committed my life to learning about and playing better golf. I've hit enough balls to know what works and what doesn't, and I want to share the benefit of that experience. You could say that this book represents the findings I have made in over 20 years of field research – the very keys that I have used to win five major championships.

In a nutshell, this book explains how I play golf. It is a practical, down-to-earth account of the way I believe a good swing takes shape, along with a keynote analysis of the related skills that you need to build a game for life. In moving through the fundamentals, developing the swing and dealing with all aspects of the short game and putting, I have tried to phrase each of the lessons as simply as possible, stressing the thoughts that I have found to be most valuable. Along the way you will find many of my ideas supported with drills and exercises, routines that I use in my own tournament preparation, which I know will accelerate your improvement.

Of course, words can only do so much. Your commitment to learning is the only surefire key to releasing your potential and shooting lower scores. No one can do that work for you. If this book inspires you to work on your game, then I have fulfilled my desire. But to sustain your improvement at this game you need a coach, a source of encouragement and feedback. Someone to trust. If you should choose to seek out a teacher, and I recommend you do, commit yourself to a series of lessons, just like I did as a boy. Give the pro a chance to get to know you, and understand your needs and aspirations. That way, you will both enjoy the learning experience.

Reading and experimenting with the thoughts contained within these pages will make you a better, a more complete, golfer. I'm certain of that.

1
MY KEY
THOUGHTS

A good swing is fluent from start to finish.
The key is to develop a series of moves that gel together
to produce a flowing chain-reaction.

I played the most consistent golf of my career to date to win the Open Championship at St Andrews in 1990. Through the excitement of 72 holes I hit all but two greens in regulation figures, and three putted just once. My victory at Muirfield in 1987 had been one long, hard grind, but around the Old Course I finally produced the sort of golf that I had always dreamed of playing in a major. My swing ran like clockwork; I felt as though I had the ball on the end of a string.

That week was significant for another reason. Out on the range just days before the championship got underway I started to condense some of my key swing thoughts into simple 'triggers'. I came up with three or four in all. They helped to keep my mind focused, and as a result I was able to control my emotions and repeat my swing, even under pressure. Of course, swing thoughts come and go, but over the years I have found that I keep coming back to tried and trusted favourites. These are my *key thoughts*, and they capture the very essence of the swing I have worked for – the swing I now want to teach you.

As you work through this book and find out more about the way a good swing works, certain words and phrases will stick in your mind, and you must use these to inspire your own chain reaction. Ultimately, your goal is to develop a swing that is as simple as it is effective; a swing that virtually ticks along by itself.

AROUND THE OLD COURSE AT ST ANDREWS I FINALLY PRODUCED THE SORT OF GOLF THAT I HAD ALWAYS DREAMED OF PLAYING IN A MAJOR.

AT ADDRESS – *knees*

My number one thought at address – *knees.* This simply reminds me to flex and brace my knees until I feel a strong, athletic tension in each thigh. If my lower body is a powerful suspension unit – and that's a pretty good image to keep in mind – then my knees are the sensitive shock absorbers that instil balance. During the swing itself, I use them to resist the turning motion of my upper body, just as if I were winding a spring.

Once I'm ready to go, I usually waggle the clubhead a couple of times to free my body of tension, and also to get a feeling for the correct arm and wrist action at the start of the swing.

THE TAKEAWAY – *rotate and set*

To capitalize on the sensation of a good waggle, I try to get the clubhead swinging early in my backswing with a synchronized arm, wrist and body action. Everything is linked together.

I work on the principle that my wrists should be fully hinged – or *set* – by the time my left arm reaches the horizontal in the backswing, and to get there I make a conscious effort to *rotate* my left forearm in a clockwise direction as I move the clubhead away from the ball. This might sound very complicated, but if you rehearse these moves in front of a mirror you will find they gel together quite easily.

I believe this position holds the key to my game. From here, all I have to do to complete my backswing is continue to turn my shoulders and upper body over the foundation of my hips and knees.

TO THE TOP – *turn*

. . . and here's the proof. As long as I rotate my left arm and set my wrists correctly to reach that critical midway point in the backswing, a full shoulder turn is all that is needed to achieve this solid on-line position at the top.

My key backswing thought, *turn*, inspires the bigger muscles in the upper body to take over and carry the club all the way to this fully coiled position. Using my right knee as a firm brace, I have simply turned my shoulders through 90 degrees, and my back faces the target. That's all you need to do.

THE TRANSITION – *slow and unwind*

Having wound the spring, it's time to let it go.

For every golfer, the great danger lies in hurrying the transition at the top, and for that reason my key thought here is *slow and unwind*. Experience has taught me that when I give myself time to make a good swing, I'll probably make one; if I rush things from the top I can kiss the shot goodbye.

Whenever I find myself under pressure I consciously remind myself to slow everything down and let the sequence unfold naturally. At my best, I might almost appear to be swinging in slow motion. What you must remember is that building acceleration is a gradual process – speed only matters at impact, and that's where your focus must be.

IMPACT – *watch it*

Old advice, and still the best. Approaching and through impact, my key thought, *watch it*, makes me focus my attention on the back of the ball.

I don't mind a slight lateral movement of the head in the backswing. If anything, that encourages a good full shoulder turn. But in the downswing I try to keep my head dead still and my spine angle steady as my body unwinds. That helps to guard against my getting too far ahead of the shot. For a precise strike, I simply *watch it* as my shoulders open up towards the target and my arms accelerate the clubhead *through* the ball.

THE FINISH – *low hands*

And so to the follow through. My key thought, *low hands*, helps me to achieve this compact, rounded position, with my right shoulder the closest part of my body to the target. Pulled around by the momentum of the clubhead, I make sure that I rotate my body all the way to the finish, so that I end up with my chest facing the target. As I complete my swing my shoulders are virtually level, and my hands end up comfortably placed behind my neck. My spine is virtually straight, and as my knees work gently together my weight is balanced on my left side. A perfect conclusion.

RÉSUMÉ

That's a brief introduction to the way in which I maintain my swing. I usually focus on just two key thoughts at a time, one for the backswing and one for the downswing. Once you find a couple of swing thoughts that work, you can – and should – use them to control your rhythm. Speak the words aloud when you practise. I often string together a short phrase such as *turn and watch it* as I hit balls, and pretty soon I have a good rhythm going. So fill your mind with these distinct images. Simple thoughts are easy to grasp. Better still, they are easy to repeat.

2

FUNDAMENTAL LESSONS

The harder I work on my swing, the more I appreciate the
fundamentals that shape it. I probably spend more time
fine-tuning the quality of my grip and set-up position
than I do checking anything else.

The first thing that determines how easily you are able to build and repeat a sound swing is the quality of your grip and set-up position: the fundamentals of golf. In the long run, the success you can expect to enjoy out on the golf course rests with the respect you have for the basic principles of the game.

Faced with that reality, the temptation may very well be to skim through this chapter and look for other more interesting lessons elsewhere, but that's a guaranteed three-putt. Unless you are prepared to work on the lessons set forward over the following pages, and set aside some time to work on the related details of grip, alignment and posture, there is really nothing this book can teach you. These disciplines hold the key to my swing, and they are equally critical to yours.

I once figured it out that over 75 per cent of my practice time revolves around either sharpening my short game – chipping, putting and bunker skills – or polishing the nuts and bolts of grip, posture and alignment that effectively hold my swing together. This is typical of the professional approach, one geared towards solid ball-striking and low scoring. With a club by your side, work on these fundamental lessons as often as you can. Repetition is the key. Study the routines that I follow – copy me – and check the details of your own set-up position in front of a mirror.

THE GRIP –
a good swing hinges on it

A sound grip makes for a secure coupling between you and the club. That is its most obvious function, but your grip is a subtle instrument.

With a sense of control must come a sense of freedom. That coupling must be flexible enough for your wrists to hinge without restriction to create a pure swinging motion. Your hands must be encouraged to work as a unit, joined together in such a way that they are able to conduct great clubhead speed with a driver one minute, and a delicate touch with a wedge the next. So a good grip is versatile in the extreme.

I am often asked how important the grip pressure is to the overall workings of the swing, and the simple answer is it means everything. I play my best golf when my arms and shoulders feel soft and syrupy, and that sensation stems directly from the pressure I exert in my hands. It all boils down to balancing feel with control. The ideal grip pressure is one that enables you to forge a close working relationship with the clubhead; you have to be able to feel it, move it, waggle it and – ultimately – control it.

Just remember that tension is a killer. As soon as you tighten your hold on the club you create a muscular gridlock in your wrists, forearms and shoulders. Inevitably, this destroys any hope you may have of making – and repeating – a good and free swing.

FITTING THE LEFT HAND –
promote the hinge

One of the dangers when placing your left hand on the club is running the shaft too high in the palm. That causes all sorts of trouble because it effectively leaves you with a grip that won't hinge properly.

To get around that problem, I find that hanging my left arm down by my side and laying the club in the fingers, which you will notice tend to curl inwards, encourages me to set the club low in the palm and more in the fingers – a natural, healthy balance. I make sure that the leading edge of the clubface and the back of my left hand are parallel, and the shaft runs diagonally through the first joint of the forefinger to a point just below the root of my little finger.

Whether or not you adopt this exact procedure, at least make sure the club is similarly placed before closing your hand. As your fingers curl around the shaft, your thumb should then rest comfortably on top, just to the right of centre.

I secure my left hand grip with the last three fingers, effectively trapping the club against the fleshy pad at the base of my thumb. My little finger, in particular, entwines itself firmly around the shaft, and that seems to bond all three together.

On a specific note, I prefer to keep my left thumb 'short' on the grip, and would encourage you to do the same. In my experience, a short left thumb, as opposed to one extended loosely down the shaft, is more effective in terms of creating leverage in the swing, and also makes for an easier task in fitting the right hand.

You should now be able to hinge your wrist and waggle the clubhead freely without any loosening of the fingers on your left hand. Remember, for optimum feel and clubhead control, you should squeeze firmly, but never too tightly.

Now, raise the club up in front of your body and check your grip position face-on. There should be a slight cupping evident at the back of your left wrist, and at least two knuckles visible on the back of your hand. The V that is formed between the thumb and forefinger should be angled to a point between your chin and your right ear.

These are the vital signs of what is known as a neutral left-hand grip. Theoretically, this is the ideal, but in practice there is scope for a little personal interpretation. A number of very good professionals prefer to use a slightly stronger version, and indeed you may find that placing your hand a hair to the right of this neutral position better suits your game.

A stronger grip is certainly preferable to a weaker one. Turning your hand clockwise on the club, so that between two and a half to three knuckles are exposed, promotes the rotation of your left forearm at the start of the backswing, and also encourages your left wrist to hinge correctly. It's up to you to experiment; just be sure to stay within these accepted parameters. And keep that hinge oiled with a light sensitive grip.

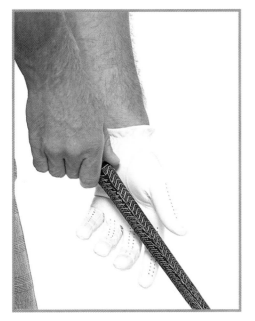

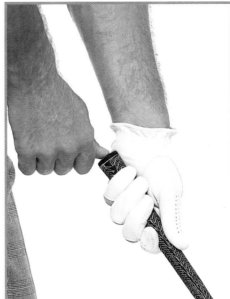

FROM A NATURAL STANDING POSITION, LAY THE CLUB IN THE FINGERS OF YOUR LEFT HAND, AND AS YOU SECURE YOUR HOLD, CHECK THAT YOUR LEFT THUMB RESTS COMFORTABLY TO THE RIGHT OF CENTRE ON TOP OF THE GRIP.

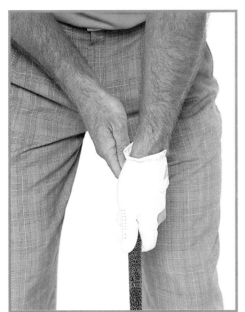

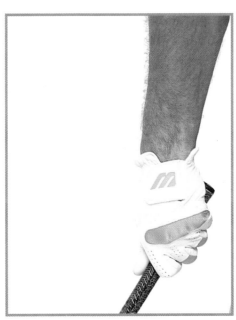

Fitting the Right Hand –
palm mirrors the clubface

Uppermost in my mind when fitting the right hand is making sure that the palm of my hand is perfectly square to the clubface, just as I expect it to be at impact. With my fingers spread, the right hand covers and fits against the left like a piece of a jigsaw. The club rests in the channel that is created as the second and third fingers curl under the shaft – these are the key pressure points on your right hand – while the left thumb has a ready-made niche beneath the fleshy pad at the base of the right thumb. To enhance this snug feeling, I exert a little downward pressure from the lifeline on my right hand on top of the left thumb. That seals my grip nicely.

How you choose to join your hands together is a matter of personal preference. I favour the overlapping Vardon grip, whereby the little finger on the right hand rides piggy-back on the left, nestling in the ridge that is created between the first and second

WITH THE FINGERS SPREAD, YOUR RIGHT HAND FITS LIKE A JIGSAW. AS YOU COMPLETE YOUR GRIP, HOOK THE RIGHT FOREFINGER AROUND THE SHAFT - 'TRIGGER' IT INTO POSITION. THAT'S YOUR GUARANTEE OF FEEL.

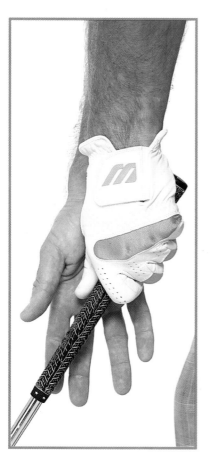

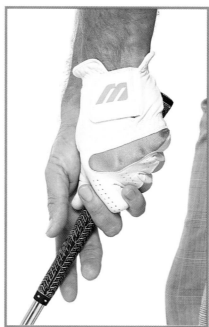

fingers. This is the pros' choice; it makes for a grip that promotes a good feel, and at the same time encourages the hands to work as a cohesive unit.

As an alternative, entwining the little finger of the right hand with the forefinger on the left – known as the interlock – is often preferred by players who have small fingers. Jack Nicklaus has used this grip his entire career, so don't let anyone tell you it doesn't work. I like the Vardon grip for the simple reason that it helps to keep my hands passive throughout the swing, but you must decide which style feels most comfortable for you.

With your hands suitably joined, complete your grip by triggering the right forefinger into position, hooking it around the shaft until it lightly brushes the tip of your right thumb. In so doing, immediately you should be struck by the sensitivity in your right hand. Waggle the clubhead back and forth and you will appreciate this potential for power and control. Remember, your right hand mirrors the clubface. It's your primary source of feel. Try to maintain a fairly light, silky pressure between your right forefinger and thumb. A good hand action demands it.

THE PALMS OF YOUR HANDS SHOULD BE FACING, THE PALM OF YOUR RIGHT HAND SQUARE WITH THE CLUBFACE, YOUR GRIP SUCH THAT THE MUSCLES IN YOUR WRISTS AND FOREARMS ARE RELAXED AND READY FOR ACTION.

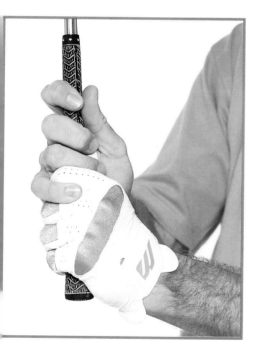

The Vardon, or Overlapping grip

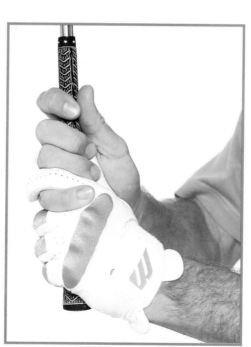

The Interlock

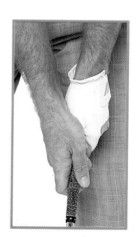

Finally, with your grip made, raise the club to a 45-degree angle and run through the following checklist.

• The back of your left hand and the palm of your right are square to the clubface.
• Your palms are parallel.
• The Vs that have been formed between thumb and forefinger of each hand point up between your chin and your right ear. These lines run approximately parallel.
• Neither hand dominates the other.
• Your grip is secured with pressure felt mainly in the last three fingers on the left hand, countered by the middle fingers and the trigger unit on the right.
• You are in control of the clubhead – it cannot easily be dislodged – but at the same time the muscles in your wrists and forearms are relaxed.

Work on forming and re-forming your grip as often as you can. Even five minutes a day is worthwhile. Keep a club by your desk at work; practise while you watch TV. As I've said before, repetition is the key to consistency.

If you have struggled with a doubtful grip for some time, making a change, no matter how small, is going to feel terrible to begin with. There's no way around that. But if you go through the motions of placing your hands together on the club often enough, making a good grip will become a natural part of your pre-shot routine. And one fewer thing to worry about on the course.

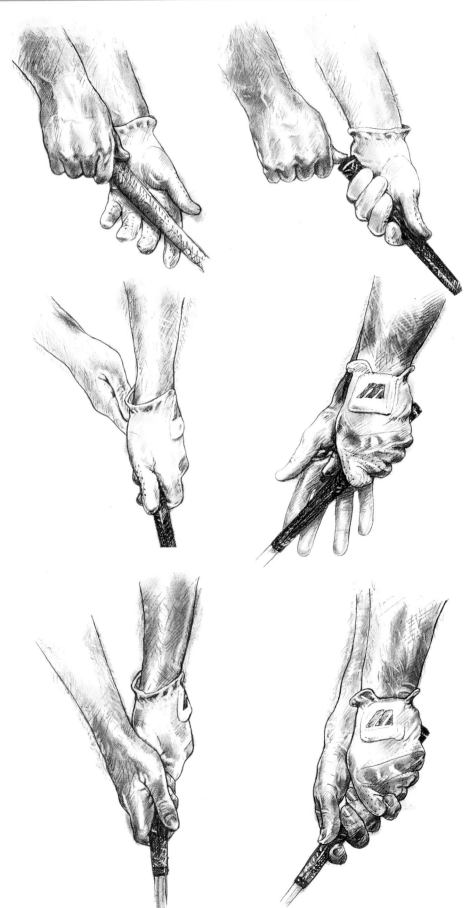

FORMING A GOOD
GRIP IS AN ART, BUT
WITH PATIENCE – AND
PRACTICE – YOU CAN
MAKE IT SECOND
NATURE.

THE SET-UP – *primed for accuracy and control*

I am meticulous in my pre-shot preparation. You have to be. The majority of swing faults can be traced to a careless mistake at address, so why not eliminate that uncertainty? It's common sense, really. Before you can hope to build a powerful, repeating swing, you must first know how to create an effective base, and then create it *every* time.

Many people I meet on my travels around the world complicate what is a very simple issue. I see players who tie themselves in knots before they even think about placing the club behind the ball. So before we look at building a good posture and set-up position, let me clear up one or two potential problem areas. I should add that everything you read from now on is subject to personal interpretation. These are solid parameters that I believe you should work within. We are all of varied height, build and flexibility, and so in certain areas a slight adjustment – it might only be half an inch either way – could suit you. Never be afraid to experiment.

The principle of parallel alignment

First, your alignment; the easiest of the fundamentals to work on, but probably the most often abused. Clearly, a good swing is going nowhere unless it is aimed in the right direction, and the golden rule to remember as you set up to the ball is that *everything you do resolves around the position of the clubface.* Your body takes its orders from there.

It works like this. Assuming a straight shot, you simply aim the leading edge of the clubface dead along the ball-to-target line, and then adjust your stance until your feet, knees, hips and shoulders fall square to that line. In the correct position, your body is now what is known as being *parallel left* of the target line.

Read that again. It's important.

The best way to appreciate this principle of alignment is to picture a set of railway tracks homing in on the flag. The outer rail corresponds with the ball-to-target line, while the inner parallel rail indicates the line your body should follow. When I practise I usually lay a couple of clubs down on the ground to help me keep a check on the position of my body, and you should do the same. Create your own set of 'tracks', and leave them there as you work on your set-up routine. Think about what you are trying to achieve. Don't stand there and simply drag one ball in after another. That defeats the object. Instead, learn to approach each shot afresh. Take aim, first with the clubface, and then with your body. You can even rehearse this at home. Do whatever it takes to groove the sensation of perfect parallel alignment.

You will find that you easily maintain a square body position when you learn to swivel your head to view the target. Don't lift your head to get a view of the hole, that threatens your entire posture. Turn your head about the natural axis of your spine, so that you look 'under' the play line.

A GOOD SET-UP IS
DESIGNED TO PLACE
YOUR BODY IN A
POSITION TO ROTATE
CORRECTLY, AND
AFFORDS YOU THE
CLEARANCE THAT IS
NECESSARY TO SWING
AND RELEASE THE
CLUBHEAD FREELY
DOWN THE TARGET
LINE. REMEMBER, AT
ADDRESS YOU ARE
GEARING YOURSELF UP
FOR IMPACT – THE
MOMENT OF TRUTH.

THE STANCE AND BALL POSITION

What's the ideal width of stance? I get asked that important question a lot. Clearly, there's a balance to be struck here between *stability* and *mobility*. If you stand with your feet spread too far apart you inhibit your ability to turn correctly; on the other hand, if your stance is too narrow you run the risk of losing your balance during the swing.

The ideal stance is one that allows you to rotate your body correctly and shift your weight back and forth with a pure swinging motion. It will vary according to the club you are using. With a driver, the longest of all clubs, I set up with my feet spread to the full width of my shoulders, and play the ball somewhere between the big toe and the heel of my left foot. That's about a two-inch span. I turn my right foot out by about ten degrees, the left by approximately twice that amount. That's all you need to encourage good footwork and achieve a full, powerful body turn.

With the driver, such a stance gives me a good anchored base to work with, while the ball position promotes the upward sweeping motion that I look for to flight my tee-shots with a low, penetrating trajectory.

But the driver is a special case. For the majority of my full shots I set up with the insides of my heels no further apart than the width of my shoulders. That's a useful benchmark. Moving through the shorter irons, from the 6-iron through to the wedge, I then work on a sliding scale, and draw my right foot in a hair towards the left with every step down. The ball position, however, remains constant, played from a point approximately two inches inside my left heel. That corresponds with the flat spot at the bottom of my swing, and so helps me to strike my shots crisply, without taking too much of a divot.

Let me stress again that these are merely guidelines, not hard and fast rules. Once you have the makings of a good set-up position, you must experiment with the width of your stance until you find the flat spot in your own swing. A simple way to do that is to make a number of practice swings on a nicely cut piece of fairway until you can identify the point at which the clubhead first strikes the ground. Use that information to determine your ideal ball position, one that rewards you with a consistent flight pattern with every club in the bag.

Driver

5-iron

9-iron

A SIMPLE ROUTINE FOR A PERFECT POSTURE

When I joined David Leadbetter in 1985 it came as quite a shock to me that I had to work so hard on rebuilding my posture, but I soon understood why. The body angles you create at address determine the quality of your pivot and ultimately they decide your ability to turn about a consistent axis. That's the very essence of a repeating swing.

Being a fairly tall player – 6′ 3″ out of my spikes – I have to monitor my posture very closely. The key is to set up the same way every time, so that you can concentrate on learning to make one swing, and one swing only. I used the following exercise for several weeks under David's eye, and I still use it today whenever I need to get back to the basics. Take a mid-iron, make your grip, and use the following four-step routine to get an idea of what a good posture feels like.

1. With the insides of your feet spread to the width of your shoulders, stand up straight and have your arms comfortably extended in front of your body.
2. Flex your knees until you feel a springy tension in each thigh, stick your rear end out a little and sense that your weight is balanced on the balls of your feet.
3. Bend gently from the hips until the sole of the club touches the ground. The upper part of each arm should now be resting lightly on your chest.
4. Perk the whole of your left side up slightly, and at the same time relax the right side of your body – let it soften and kink in.

My guess is that this position feels totally alien to you, and about as likely to produce a good swing as standing on your head. That's how I felt for a while, but it gets better with practice. Repetition has its rewards, and as you become more familiar with the sensation of a good posture you will find that you begin to adopt this position more naturally.

PREPARING FOR ACTION – *routine business*

Following a carefully rehearsed routine is the best defence mechanism you can have under pressure; it gives you something positive to focus on, no matter how hairy the situation may be. The ultimate reward to all your hard work behind the scenes is if, out on the golf course, you are able to switch to auto-pilot, and good golf is then all about going through the motions.

This is the way I go about playing a typical shot.

My pre-shot routine actually starts long before I reach the ball; as I walk to the tee or down a fairway I'm constantly aware of the changing conditions. My senses are alive to the elements, the trouble spots on that hole and the general lie of the land. Once I arrive at the ball I have a pretty good idea of the shot I intend to play, but to set the wheels in motion I usually stand a couple of yards back and try to visualize the flight of the ideal shot in my mind. That's a vivid image, not a blurred guess.

Address the shot, not the ball – I don't remember where I first heard that advice, but it's right on the button.

Some people debate on whether you should grip the club and then aim it, or aim it and then grip it. Frankly, it doesn't matter. All you should be interested in as you walk to the ball is aiming the clubface squarely on the target and getting your feet, knees, hips and shoulders aimed *parallel left* of that line.

Once I'm satisfied with my alignment, I work on building my posture from the ground up. I take my stance, check the ball position in relation to the width between my heels, and then flex my knees until I can feel a springy tension in each thigh. It's a fairly basic image to keep in mind, but I often try to visualize the structure of the Eiffel Tower, just to remind myself of the need to create a good, stable base with my lower body. My feet, knees and thighs represent the lower level of the tower. The muscles are keyed up to support the coiling of my torso. To enhance this feeling I push out with the insides of my knees, and that braces the legs.

Another way to describe this sensation is that it's similar to the feeling I might have if I were about to dive into a pool. My weight is slightly forwards, on the balls of my feet, and my legs are lively.

To complete my posture I bend gently from the hips, stick my rear-end out, and let my arms hang freely down. The lower part of my back is now comfortably straight, the upper back nicely rounded. In order to assume its rightful position on the grip, my right hand naturally has to reach down a little further than the left, and that gives me a comfortable slant across the shoulders. With the left side of my body perked slightly up, I then try to relax the whole of my right side, and let it kink in just a fraction. That makes for a nice feeling of being behind the shot, and encourages a good weight shift at the start of the backswing.

The tendency for many people – me included – is sometimes to get a little too crouched over the ball. To guard against that happening I often murmur the words *tall and straight* as I settle into position. I like to feel that I dominate the ball at address. You have to let it know who's the boss.

Finally, I keep my chin up so that my shoulders have room to turn, and take a couple of deep breaths to expand the chest fully. That makes for a proud, robust position. When you follow this procedure, your body should feel passive, but at the same time bouncy and alert.

Here's the acid test. When you check your profile in front of a mirror, a line dropped vertically from the middle of your right shoulder should touch the front of your right knee on its way down and through the ball of your right foot. You should look for this guarantee with every club in the bag; it's a sure sign of good, athletic balance. All the muscles in your body are now geared up to work together in the swing.

I often wonder how many millions of times I have gripped and set up to a ball. Tens of millions, probably. And yet I still check my address position religiously every time I play or practise. One or two key words help to keep me on track. I might think *knees*, or *tall and straight*, simple reminders that help me to achieve a good, athletic position.

In Chapter 1, I emphasized *knees* as one of my key thoughts. I really cannot stress too strongly the role of the knees in terms of your ability to create good body angles at address. In my mind, the key to adopting a good posture is to

use your knees as pistons, and adjust your height to maintain a fairly consistent spine angle with every club in the bag. Out on the course your set-up position must be versatile enough to cope with all manner of awkward slopes and lies, and again your knees hold the key. You must flex them, bounce up and down on them, and learn to create an all-round sense of liveliness in the lower body. Feel the lie of the ground through your feet, and adjust your set up according to what your senses tell you.

Finally, the waggle. It has become my trademark over the years. Someone once told me that my swing was nothing more than a big waggle carried to the top with a good body turn. That's a pretty good description.

I first began to appreciate the real importance of a good waggle during the Open at Muirfield in 1987. Those were the early days of learning to set my wrists correctly in the backswing, and I had to make a conscious effort to get that clubhead swinging away from the ball early. I made two waggles, and then I was off. Now it's a habit. Used correctly, the waggle *is* a mini-swing, a sneak preview of what's about to come. It's an opportunity for you to rehearse the correct wrist action and remind all the muscles in your body of the way in which you intend to initiate your backswing movement.

No great player has ever moved from a rock-solid position at address. Everyone has a pressure release, a personal quirk or mannerism that helps them to relax and start their swing smoothly. Jack Nicklaus is known for turning his head gently to the right; Gary Player triggers his swing with the right knee; Tom Watson makes a brisk waggle, and then everything 'fires'.

You have to find your own trigger. Personally, I like to waggle the clubhead a couple of times to free my body of tension. It's part and parcel of a set-up position that exudes motion.

3

BUILDING A
SWING FOR LIFE

I simplify the backswing to a three-step sequence.
It is my sincere belief that anyone who has the discipline
to learn and make natural this series of movements has
the ability to become a single-figure golfer.

When I made the decision to rebuild my swing in 1985 it was not uncommon for me to spend eight hours a day on the practice tee. Now, older and wiser, I have such a thorough understanding of the mechanics involved that I can focus on certain key moves and capture the essence of a repeating method with just a handful of drills and exercises – the benefit of a good education.

The ability to conjure up these drills is David Leadbetter's trademark. With a shrewd understanding of the way we best learn, David uses these exercises to simplify theory and communicate that elusive element of 'feel'. It works, believe me. In a typical warm-up session I might hit 30 balls with one drill, then 30 with another, and that's it. I'm ready to go out and play. The bonus is that the time I save working on my long game I can use to polish my short game skills on and around the putting green. And no matter how good your ball-striking might be, that's where your performance as a golfer will ultimately be judged.

This chapter represents the key findings I have made in all my years of field research. I have spared you the intricate and unnecessary details. What follows is all the theory you need to build a solid golf swing, and each stage along the way is supported with the drills that I use in my day-to-day preparation. If you are anything like me, the excitement of working on these lessons and gradually improving the quality and consistency of your ball-striking will be tantamount to an addiction.

But before we set to work, let me draw your attention to one important truth. Still images tend to disguise the silky flow of a good golf swing. *Don't ever lose sight of the fact that the positions you see illustrated here are snapshots of a free-flowing motion.* Digest this information and use the various drills to work on each of the individual-links in the chain. But above all, concentrate on fusing these links together with a sense of elegance and rhythm.

THE SET-UP – *primed and ready for action*

This is often thought of as a static position, but that's not the way I see it. A good set up is dynamic and always promises a coordinated, athletic movement. Now is a time for your brain to be sending out messages to the body; route maps reminding all your muscles what you hope to achieve with the swing. Having pictured the shot, you ought to be able to see the flight of the ball in your mind's eye.

The pre-swing checks that I make revolve around the basics. There's no getting away from them. I carefully align the leading edge of the clubface along the ball-to-target line, and then keep that point of reference in focus as I shuffle my body into position. Similarly, you must cultivate a series of good habits that add up to guarantee a workable stance and posture. Remember, *your feet, knees, hips and shoulders should run parallel with the target line.* Crooked alignment leads to a crooked swing, but if you keep that image of the railway tracks in your mind, you won't go far wrong.

I make no apologies for the fact that I continue to stress the importance of posture and the set-up position generally. The angles you create with your body at address, and specifically your spine angle, determine the axis about which you turn and dictate your ability to pivot correctly. So they had better be right.

Remember, *a vertical line descending from the middle of your right shoulder should touch the right knee on its way down into the ball of your right foot.* That's a sure sign of balance and poise, and you should use it to check your posture with every club in the bag.

As far as the distribution of your weight is concerned, I believe in a fairly even spread between each foot. Certainly, I don't intend to confuse the issue with a meaningless ratio. If anything, perhaps favour your right side a little more than your left to accentuate the natural slant across the shoulders. But don't overdo it. The most important thing is that your weight is centred on the balls of your feet, ready to flow back and forth with the progression of your swing.

I've said it before and I'll say it again: one of the best ways to achieve a good posture is to think about your knees. I often remind myself to stand *tall and straight*, then flex my knees until I feel that my lower body is braced. The muscles in your legs must feel strong and *lively*, ready to support the powerful coiling of your upper body.

Finally, when all systems are ready to go, waggle the clubhead a couple of times to rid your hands, arms and shoulders of any lingering tension. Whatever your swing trigger is, when you give the signal to move, everything should now be geared up to move away *together*.

DRILL

Trap a beach-ball, and *feel* your knees

I make no secret of the fact that I tend to focus on my knees more than anything else as I set up to the ball. All I am interested in is creating and maintaining a firm base upon which to make a good swing, and the knees hold the key. I use the beach-ball drill from time to time to remind myself of the need to keep the legs braced from address to the top of the backswing. It's easy. You simply trap the ball between your knees, then squeeze it and keep it there as you coil your upper body.

Keep this exercise in mind and come back to it from time to time as you work on building your swing. It will serve to remind you of the sensation of keeping the distance between your knees fairly constant, and so encourages a strong leg action and a powerful backswing coil.

THIS 'SET' POSITION
HOLDS THE KEY TO MY
GAME. AS LONG AS I
REACH THIS HALFWAY
CHECKPOINT,
COMPLETING MY
SHOULDER TURN
GIVES ME A SOLID
BACKSWING. SUCH
SIMPLICITY IS YOUR
ULTIMATE GOAL.

THE BACKSWING –
setting up a chain reaction

A good swing is fluent from start to finish; it's a chain reaction in which one good move can be seen to lead to another. The key to repeating such a swing lies in timing the movement of your hands and arms with the rotation of your body right from the word 'go'.

To set off a truly coordinated motion, I work on what is known as an *early wrist set*. In other words, I expect my wrists to be fully hinged – and the club 'set' on plane – by the time my hands reach waist high. From then on, all I have to worry about is turning the bigger muscles in my body and completing my pivot to arrive at a solid backswing position. That's the real beauty of this method.

To accelerate the learning process, I have simplified the key moves that I make in the backswing down to a three-step sequence. *It is my sincere belief that anyone who has the discipline to learn and make natural this series of movements has the potential to become a single-figure golfer.* With a mid-iron, work on these specific positions and polish each move until you are ready to add the next. And remember, your goal is to blend these three moves together so finely that you end up with a pure, swinging motion.

1. Turn everything away together

A good swing is either bought or sold in the first move away from the ball. For a consistent shape and tempo, the key is to get everything moving and working *together*.

In front of a mirror, focus on turning the club, your arms, shoulders and stomach away from the ball in one synchronized movement. By the time your hands reach a position above the middle of your right thigh, the clubhead should point to 8 o'clock on an imaginary clockface. Rehearse this in slow motion. As everything turns away from the ball, feel your weight move over on to the right side. Let it 'bump' across, and feel the build-up of tension in your right thigh. To the outsider it might not be apparent that your weight has moved at all, but you should be aware of gradually increasing the pressure on the ball of your right foot. Here's a useful tip. At address, feel that you exert a slight pressure on your chest with the upper part of your left arm, and then maintain that pressure as you turn and make this first move in the backswing. As long as you keep your hands and wrists passive, the clubhead will work away low to the ground and trace the desired inside path, just as it should.

When you achieve a perfectly coordinated one-piece takeaway for the first time, you might think that the clubface is fanning open as you move it away from the ball. That's just an illusion. *The clubface is simply turning in harmony with the rotation of your body.* It is perfectly square to the path of your swing.

NO SIGN OF ANY TENSION, NO UNNECESSARY 'SNATCHING' OF THE CLUBHEAD. A GOOD FIRST MOVE SYNCHRONIZING SHOULDERS, ARMS AND CLUB.

DRILL

Rotate the club as you rotate your body

The exercise you see here will help you to appreciate the sensation of rotation and 'togetherness' that you should have as you move the club away from the ball.

It works like this. Adopt your normal stance, then grip down the shaft of a mid-iron until the butt-end of the club rests in your belly button. Now rehearse your takeaway. Focus on turning your stomach and the club in tandem until you reach that 8 o'clock position. No further. If you fail to maintain the correct linkage between the movement of your arms and the turning of your body, the club will work loose.

Repeat this exercise until you are able to synchronize the movement of the club and your body every time. Then with that feeling fresh in your mind, revert to a normal grip and groove your takeaway in the regular fashion.

2. Hinge your wrists to set the club on plane

Now that you have forged that all-important first link in the chain, let's turn our attention to the subtle hand and wrist action that you need in order to swing the club on the correct plane.

Rehearse this in front of a mirror. Moving through the 8 o'clock position, rotate your left forearm gently away from the ball as the right elbow softens and folds. At the same time, let your right wrist hinge back on itself, just as it would if you were to turn and shake hands with someone standing to your right. In fact that's a useful analogy: you achieve exactly the right position if, from address, you simply turn to shake hands – *'How do you do?'* Your left arm will be forced to move across and rotate correctly.

The next important checkpoint occurs as the clubshaft reaches a position where it is both horizontal with the ground and parallel with the line across your toes, what you might call the 9 o'clock position. Here, the toe-end of the club should point up towards the sky (that confirms it is still square to the path of your swing), while the clubface and the back of your left hand look straight ahead. If you stop your swing here and turn to face the club, you should find that the clubface is square to your body, just as it was at address.

As your left arm continues to rotate and your backswing progresses, the full and critical hinging of the wrists occurs between the time your hands pass your right thigh and the moment your left arm reaches horizontal with the ground. (When I really am swinging the club well, I look for that 'setting' to occur sooner rather than later, ie. *before* my left arm reaches that parallel position.) The club is said to be 'on plane' when *a line extended down through the shaft strikes the ground approximately midway between your feet and the ball-to-target line*.

As your left arm reaches the horizontal, your wrists should be fully hinged and the club set on plane.

In all my years of playing golf I would say that this is the single most important guarantee I look for when I practise. The club is now 'in the slot', and everything is plugged in for impact. Provided that my lower body continues to offer a firm base, winding the bigger muscles in my shoulders and trunk will reward me with a solid position at the top and a consistent angle of attack on the ball.

To all intents and purposes, *if you can achieve this fully set position on a regular basis, you've cracked it*. Once the club is on plane, all you have to do is complete your body turn for a full and powerful backswing coil. Work on this connection between your arm swing and your body turn until it becomes a natural movement; groove these moves in front of a mirror. In the fully set position, your hands should appear opposite the right side of your chest, as you look to the right. Another exercise I use will help you. Trap a headcover under the upper part of your left arm, and keep it there as you reach this three-quarter position. If it should fall free, then your arms are working *independently* of your body. You need to focus a little harder on rotating your left forearm at the start of the backswing, and grow accustomed to the sensation of your left arm working *across* your chest.

Get the clubhead swinging early

As my swing has evolved I have tended to focus more on the fully set position and less on the earlier takeaway checkpoints we have covered. In time, you should do the same. While it's important that you know how to start your swing correctly, step-by-step, more valuable is blending together these moves in one continuous fluent motion.

The key is to get the clubhead *swinging early*, and this drill helps you with a running start. Move the club several feet into the follow through, almost to waist high, then let it fall and swing like a pendulum. As long as you keep the muscles in your hands and arms relaxed, you should find that your wrists begin to respond naturally to the momentum of the clubhead, and you arrive at the halfway position in one continuous motion.

When I do this I sometimes say out loud the words 'rotate…and…set' in time with the swing. That helps my rhythm. I might do this a dozen times in a practice session. Then, satisfied that my wrists are hinging correctly and the club is on plane, I go ahead and hit shots with a full swing.

I haven't made mention of the legs, and really you don't need to think about what's going on down below once you have made that initial bump across to the right side. The key is to maintain the flex in your right knee, so the muscles in your right thigh absorb the transfer of weight. Assuming that you set up to the ball correctly in the first place, your legs will be forced to respond as you turn your upper body on the target. That left knee will tend to be drawn in towards the ball as you continue to turn and coil. That's quite normal. Just make sure that it doesn't shoot forwards or work beyond your toe line.

3. STRETCH AND COIL TO THE TOP

. . . and here's the finished product. From the halfway stage I have simply turned my shoulders through 90 degrees to achieve this fully wound backswing. My left arm is comfortably placed (I make no effort to keep it straight) and still my right knee has retained the original flex that I created at address. There is a definite sense of *stretching* my upper body. I feel strong, but at the same time relaxed and in balance. Someone could give me a good nudge from behind and I wouldn't fall over.

Like a spring wound to its fullest extent, your backswing position should be one similarly loaded with energy, just itching to be released on the ball. As you reach the top you ought to be aware of increasing the tension in your right thigh. The majority of your weight should now be supported by the muscles running down the inside of your right leg. That's the feeling I have.

Don't be alarmed if you find that you need to ease your head to the right to achieve this position. Keeping your head rigid only serves to restrict the rotation of your spine, and that can lead to unnecessary (and often quite painful) strain on the lower part of the back. There has to be a certain amount of leeway.

The rear view of the swing is the most telling. When you look in the mirror, it ought to be clear that your shoulders have turned about the natural axis of your spine, while your hands and arms have simply followed the lead of the body pivot. Your right elbow should have worked its way behind your body, and the angle created by your right forearm should match the angle of your spine. The clubshaft is again parallel with the ball-to-target line, and the back of your left hand mirrors the clubface. All positive signs of a backswing that has been made in perfect plane.

One further thought. I am supple enough to turn my back on the target without raising my left heel, but you may need to let yours come off the ground. That's not a problem, but I do urge you to keep such footwork to a minimum. The important thing is that you maintain that feeling of strength and resistance in the legs.

DRILL

Strengthen the heart of your swing

I play my best golf when my swing is reduced to nothing more complicated than turning back and turning through: 'turn and turn'. That's one of the most effective swing thoughts you can have. The pivot exercise is a favourite of mine. It reminds you what a good rotary body motion feels like.

In front of a mirror, adopt a ready posture, with plenty of flex in your knees and your chin up, then hook a club through your arms behind your back and prepare to work on your pivot motion. Copy me. As you rotate your shoulders to the right, sense a stubborn resistance in your right knee so that you really do have to stretch your upper body to the fully loaded backswing position. Then, as if to make your downswing, unwind your upper body and let your head come round naturally as your shoulders rotate to face the target.

Finish with your knees comfortably together, your spine vertical and your belt buckle facing forwards. Great for your early morning stretch!

Set your wrists, then turn your body

I used this pre-set and coil routine seven days a week when I first started working with David. It really does simplify the components of a good backswing. To start, place a club on the ground parallel to and just outside your toe-line, then take your normal grip and set-up position. The object of the exercise is now to hinge your wrists to the right (keeping your hands in their original address position) until the club you are holding is parallel with the shaft on the ground. Make sure their alignment is spot on. Then, and without any further manipu-

lation of the hands, you simply turn your left shoulder under your chin and swing the club to the top of your backswing.

Check your position in the mirror. The spine angle you created at address should have been maintained, there must be no straightening or tilting, and the club should again be parallel with the target line. A solid backswing in two easy moves. As you become more ambitious, try hitting a few shots off a tee: set your wrists . . . turn your shoulders . . . and bang! That's a great confidence booster.

THE DOWNSWING – *releasing the spring*

Just as you reach the top of your swing you are starting back down. For a split second your body is actually moving in two directions at once: the left side of your body works back towards the target before your arms have completed their backswing movement. That's what creates energy, or *torque* in the swing.

Imagine throwing a ball a great distance. Even before you have wound up your body and worked your throwing hand behind you, the gears are thrown into reverse. It is that whiplash effect which maximizes the speed in your arm and wrist. The elasticity in your body catapults your release, and so it is with golf.

For a smooth, fluid transition, I focus on holding the flex in my right knee and thigh for a split second as I reach the top. My left knee and left shoulder make the first move towards the target, while the right side of my body holds momentarily. That slight delay rewards me with the opportunity then to release the whole right side of my body hard through impact. It all boils down to that magical ingredient: *timing*. The key is to work on blending the two halves of your swing so finely that you end up with one fluent, continuous motion. Think about this when you practise. Say the words out loud 'slow . . . and . . . unwind' to correspond with a smooth backswing, a subtle transition at the top and a powerful response through the ball. If you took a straw poll of the longest hitters in the professional game and asked each of them to nominate a thought for distance, I guarantee that most would say they try to swing *easier*. They give themselves time to unwind fully. Keep that in mind.

EVERYTHING THAT HAPPENS IN THE DOWNSWING HAS ITS ORIGINS IN THE BACKSWING. THE BETTER YOU WIND YOUR BODY UP, THE MORE SUCCESSFULLY YOU WILL UNWIND IT DOWN. THAT'S WHY I WORK SO HARD ON SETTING THE CLUB ON PLANE AND TURNING MY BODY CORRECTLY. A GOOD DOWNSWING IS VERY MUCH A *REFLEXIVE* ACTION.

It's interesting to note the position of the wrists approaching impact. Remember, the wrists were fully set by the time they reached the midpoint in the backswing, and as long as I continue to turn and unwind correctly they will remain in this set position deep into the downswing. Then, as the centrifugal forces unwinding the club become too great to hold back, the angle in my wrists will be forced to release, boosting clubhead speed through impact. This is not a conscious skill on my part. It is simply the reward you are due when you resist the temptation to hit too early with the hands and instead allow your downswing sequence to unfold naturally. If anything, I try to *delay* releasing the clubhead. I hold that angle in my right wrist up until the very last moment, until I can hold it no longer. The full release of the right hand actually occurs two or three feet after the ball. That's the only time in the swing both arms are fully extended.

Another thing. I don't think in terms of hitting *at* the ball. To me that places too much emphasis on the impact position itself. It assumes the swing ends there. Instead, I work around images of *squeezing* the ball off the turf, or *collecting* it as I rotate my body and release the clubhead to a full finish. When I'm striking it well, the ball simply gets in the way of a good swing. Note the key points below, but don't stand on the practice tee and sweat over meeting each of these conditions one by one. This is where the drills and exercises featured in this chapter really score. Work on them often enough and gradually you will develop a swing that rewards you with a solid impact position over and over again.

IMPACT
key points

• The head and spine are steady behind the ball.
• Having cleared and rotated from the top of the backswing, the hips and shoulders are now open in relation to the target line.
• The spine angle is virtually identical to the angle in which it was positioned at address.
• The right knee is working on a line towards the left knee – it does not shoot out towards the ball. The left leg is braced and provides a resistance to the 'hit'.

THE GREAT THING ABOUT THIS GAME IS THAT YOU EXPERIENCE SOMETHING DIFFERENT EVERY TIME YOU MAKE A SWING. WHEN YOU STRIKE THE BALL PURE OUT OF THE MIDDLE OF THE CLUBFACE, YOU WILL BE ALIVE TO A HOST OF WONDERFUL FEELINGS. SOME YOU REMEMBER, OTHERS WILL FADE. AND THAT IS WHAT BRINGS YOU BACK FOR MORE.

Learn how to release your right arm

The right arm drill will teach you the value of good timing – the essence of a pure swing. Make your backswing, then take your left hand off the club and try to make a loud swish as you make your downswing. Go ahead and zip the clubhead through impact, just as if you were clipping the tops off daisies. When you time your release correctly, the angle at your right elbow will open as your right arm swings down. That's exactly what should happen. You are not 'casting' the clubhead forwards or 'spinning' your right shoulder out, you are simply training your right arm to release and swing the club correctly.

If you want to be a little more adventurous, take a short iron and try to hit a few balls off a tee. Put your left hand behind your back, and clip each ball away with a smooth, almost lazy, right arm action. You will find this difficult to start with. I certainly did. But once you get used to associating the feeling of the right hand with the clubface through impact you will hit some nice straight shots. Punctuate your practice sessions with half a dozen one-handed shots every 20 minutes or so, and then go after that sensation of a free-flowing release with a normal swing.

DRILL

'Thumbs up' for a crisp strike

A lot of people ask me how they can improve the quality of their ball-striking, and this is what I tell them. Take your 9-iron and work on making a crisp ball-turf strike with a three-quarter swing. Think 'thumbs up' as you turn back and through. That will remind you to hinge your wrists correctly and set the club on a good plane. Then work on building up your speed. Keep your knees firm and rotate your body hard as you swing through impact. Try to make as much noise in the strike as you can. I often imagine there's a piece of sandpaper on the clubface, and then try to take the skin off the ball. I feel like I squeeze the ball into the turf, so that as I release the clubhead, it streams away.

THE FINISH – *wrap the club around your neck*

So many people neglect their follow through. Perhaps they feel that once the ball has gone there is nothing more they can do to influence its flight. That's true, I suppose, but it misses the point entirely. Remember, your follow-through position is a statement of intent, and knowing where you want to finish will help you release the clubhead correctly through impact.

The word that perhaps best sums up my downswing and follow through is commitment. Having done all the hard work to achieve a consistent backswing position, I have total trust in the shape of my downswing and fire the club through impact with absolute conviction. As I unwind to a full finish the positions that I move through are purely reflexive. Similarly, you should be roller-coasting along, your hands, arms and body pulled around by the sheer momentum of the speeding clubhead.

When I look at the details, I expect to see my body poised straight and firm. There's still a little resistance in my hips and knees to support the recoil, but basically I'm relaxed. The majority of my weight is now supported on the left leg, while the right foot is balanced on its toe, revealing the spikes on the shoe. Thanks to a strong but sensitive leg action, I could hold this position rock solid for several seconds.

You will notice that the right knee has worked in towards the left. Indeed, the knees have worked back and forth along a fairly straight line throughout the swing, and that's important.

These are the finishing touches you must look for. There should be no hint of a reverse-C, your spine should be relatively straight, and you end up with your chest facing the target. As you turn through impact it should almost feel as if someone has taken hold of your left hip pocket and pulled it sharply around and behind you.

Another useful swing thought is to focus on getting your right shoulder past your chin. If you do that you can be fairly confident that you have completed your follow through. Turn and rotate to face the target, and let your head come around with the right shoulder so that you pick up the flight of the ball. As your head turns in tandem with the spine, you should have a feeling of looking under the shot.

I often think in terms of wrapping the club around my neck, so that the shaft rests along my shirt collar. The momentum of my hands and arms pulls me round to a full finish, with my right shoulder the closest part of my body to the target. When I practise, I make my swing and hold that position until the ball drops. That's the classic pose.

DRILL

Swing Baseball style for a full finish

A lot of golfers appreciate the importance of turning fully in the backswing, but relatively few think about turning all the way through the ball as they unwind. The baseball swing encourages you to rotate your body and shift your weight correctly in both directions. Try it. Hold the club out at waist height, and imagine you are about to smash a home run. Turn your back on the target and then whistle the clubhead through impact to a full and balanced finish. All your energy should be spent. As you work on this drill, lower the clubhead to the ground in stages, but keep looking for that sensation of a full turn and a burst of acceleration through impact.

Simplify the feeling of 'rotation' and 'resistance'

The powerful coiling effect is only possible when there is a certain amount of resistance present in your swing, and this push-palm exercise is one that will help you feel the sensation in your whole body as you wind and unwind.

Take a club in your left hand and assume your normal address position, but cross your left wrist over the right, so that the back of your right hand rests against the back of your left. Now work on your swing. As you make your backswing, you should feel that your right hand is pushing the left. Keep the flex in your right knee to resist the rotation of your torso, and sense the muscles in the upper part of your back stretching like elastic as you reach the top of your swing.

Hold that position momentarily, then unwind.

In the downswing, the left hand does the pushing, and this time you turn against the resistance of the left knee. At the moment of 'impact' you should feel that the back of your left hand is facing the target, and from there your right side should fire to a full finish.

Placing your hands together in this fashion works wonders for your understanding of stretch and resistance in the golf swing. It also has the benefit of teaching you the correct rotation of both the left and right arm. That might sound complicated, but it isn't. As long as you keep the backs of your hands together you will find that your arms rotate and fold correctly. Work on this drill when you practise, and also out on the course when you need to recapture the feeling of a good swing.

4

TIMING AND TEMPO

KEYS TO CONSISTENCY

*Nothing is more important than swinging the club
at a pace you can comfortably control. I always try to
swing the club with the same easy rhythm. The greater the pressure,
the more I tell myself to slow down.*

Years ago, I remember discussing the merits of physical effort in the swing and the relative quality of my ball-striking with my first coach, Ian Connelly. We were on the practice ground at Welwyn Garden City.

As a junior, I always thought I could hit the ball further than I did. Rather than take a 4-iron, I'd always try to hit a hard five. There was an element of violence in my swing, which did little to enhance my consistency out on the course. Ian suggested a short experiment.

'*Take a dozen balls,*' he said, '*and hit six of them as hard as you can with your 5-iron.*' I did as I was told.

'*Now try to hit the remaining six with no more than three quarters of your normal effort. Feel like you swing in slow motion.*'

You can guess what happened. The more I eased off, the better I hit the ball, the sweeter it felt coming off the middle of the clubface, and the straighter it flew. In that instant I learned perhaps the most important lesson of my career, and a languid rhythm has been my trademark ever since. While my swing has changed over the years, my tempo – or at least the *consistency* of my tempo – has remained constant. This is something I regard as being fundamental to the learning process.

TEMPO – *a personal characteristic*

All great players have the discipline to swing every club in the bag at a relatively even pace, or *tempo*. Some are faster than others, which is only to be expected. We are all different in that respect. But slow or fast, the controlled golfer has a rhythm that runs like a major vein all the way through his game.

Ever since that discovery I made as a junior, I have always preferred to swing the club with a fairly slow, unhurried tempo. I could hit a few balls with a 3-wood, then change to a 5-iron, and you would hardly notice a difference in the speed of my swing or the amount of effort I put into the shot. I trust the club to do its job and concentrate on making a good turn away from and through the ball. The greater the pressure, the more I tell myself to calm my swing.

That was another lesson I learned early in my competitive career. When the heat is on, most players tend to quicken their step and their movements over the ball. Inevitably, they lose the thread that holds their swing together. If you are aware of these signs, you can defend them, and as a 19-year-old I tested that 'slow-slow' theory to win my first major amateur title – the British Youths' Championship at Ganton. Coming down the final stretch I can remember telling myself to 'breathe deep, swing easy'. That is still the best pressure release I know.

On my travels around the world I don't see many golfers who swing the club too slowly, but I see plenty who swing it too fast, and it kills them. My advice is to watch players such as Ernie Els and Fred Couples, slow swingers who hit the ball a mile, and learn from their example. The easier you swing the club, the better you'll strike the ball. Plus, you will always have that little extra thrust in reserve when you need it.

Of course, there are exceptions, and you may be one of them. Nick Price has always played with a fast, upbeat swing, and its suits him. He walks fast, talks fast and rips through the ball like he wants to split it. But he maintains a wonderful rhythm that allows all the pieces of his swing to fall into sequence. José Maria Olazabal is another player who thrives on nervous energy and he, too, is an all-out, upbeat swinger. But like Price, his rhythm is consistent through the bag.

Consistent through the bag – there's the key.

Pay attention to the way you walk, the way you talk and general lifestyle. Be honest; don't fight your natural tempo. We all have a different 'twitch' factor of the muscles. Some of us operate better at a slow pace; others are designed to operate at a much quicker tempo. It really doesn't matter, as long as you discover your personal beat and stick with it.

EASY DOES IT – AND NO ONE DOES IT BETTER THAN FRED COUPLES, ONE OF THE GAME'S LONGEST HITTERS AND LAZIEST SWINGERS.

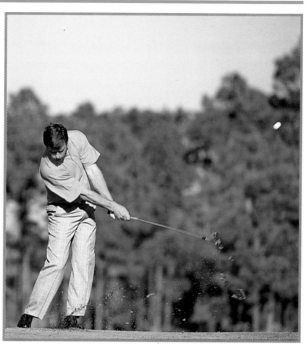

Start slowly, build on your confidence

Someone once told me a racing driver will often cycle around a new track to get a feel for all the twists and turns he has to negotiate. At a relatively slow speed, his senses can take in all the relevant information he needs to perform at a much greater speed. The same principle applies in learning a golf swing.

Repetition is the key, and like the racing driver your senses are more likely to absorb information when you take your time and listen to what your body is telling you. It's all about developing your so-called 'muscle memory'. Start slowly and build up speed gradually is my advice. If you focus on swinging the club at a realistic and comfortable pace, your confidence will grow and the links in the chain will slot into place. In practice, I will often work on a certain move in isolation. But when I get down to the business of putting all the pieces together I concentrate 100 per cent on the overall *flow* of my golf swing. My goal is to narrow the gap between the quality of my best and worst shots, so that I end up with a predictable flight pattern, and, ultimately, control of the ball. As a professional, you quickly learn that tournaments are not decided on the strength of your good shots. They are either won or lost by the number of poor shots you hit. So the key to scoring – and you can apply this to your own game – is to minimize the damage. Which is why a consistent tempo is so important.

Here are a few ideas and drills that I use in my day-to-day preparation, thoughts that enable me to keep my swing in a groove. Some of these exercises are suitable to be rehearsed at home in the garden. Hit plastic balls to ingrain your basic swing shape, and stay in touch with your rhythm and tempo in between games. Just remember that whenever I say 'slow slow' as a swing thought, my version of 'slow slow' is likely to be quite different from your own. Tempo is a personal characteristic – keep that in mind.

WHETHER I AM PLAYING A DRIVER, A 5-IRON OR A WEDGE, I ALWAYS TRY TO MAKE THE SAME UNHURRIED SWING, AND LET THE CLUB TAKE CARE OF HITTING THE BALL.

ALL ABOUT BALANCE –
swing with your feet together

This exercise is as old as the hills, but it's one of the best when it comes to capturing that feeling of your body turning and your arms swinging in harmony. I call it my Charlie Chaplin routine. With a 7-iron, stand with your feet no more than four or five inches apart, and angle your heels towards each other. Now, limit yourself to a three-quarter swing, and hit a few shots. Try to strike each ball pure out of the middle of the clubface, and see how closely you can group your shots together. With such a limited stance, the emphasis must be on turning your body and swinging the club in *balance*. There is no scope for any jerky or violent movement, so you learn to develop a good rhythm and a silky smooth, fully coordinated swing.

WITH YOUR BALANCE UNDER THREAT, THE ONLY WAY YOU CAN MAKE A GOOD SWING IS TO ENSURE A SMOOTH RHYTHM EITHER SIDE OF THE BALL.

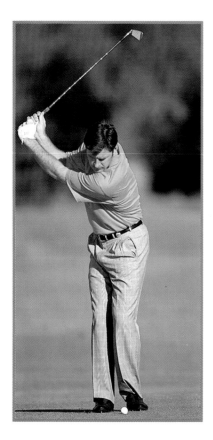
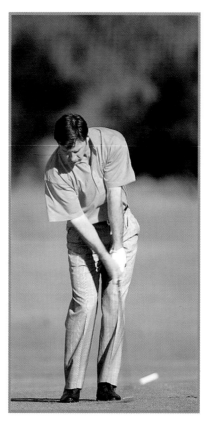
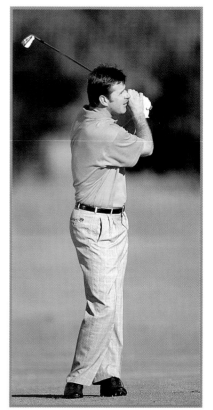

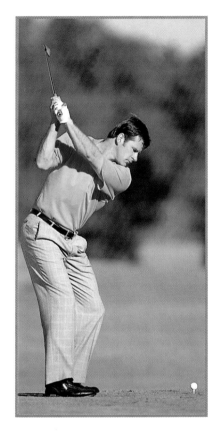
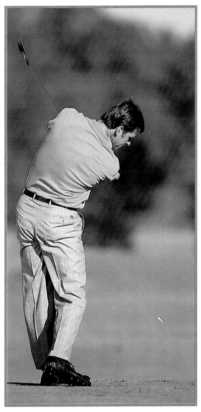

What this exercise does is encourage you to make a good hip and shoulder turn about a steady spine angle. You should sense that your weight flows back and forth with the logical progression of your swing, but your legs will barely move. I find that breathing in and breathing out in harmony with my backswing and downswing, helps to regulate the tempo of my movement; it keeps my mind focused and my body *quiet*. Use these thoughts and practise for 10 or 15 minutes, then revert to a regular stance and try to recreate that same balanced feeling. To improve the quality of your striking, tee the ball up high and try to sweep it off the peg. Make it sit about an inch off the ground, and feel that you '*collect*' the ball, as opposed to hitting at it. If you swing too hard you will probably catch it off the top of the blade, and it will feel horrible. So make yourself think 'slow', and let the clubhead meet the ball square on.

FOR A BETTER SENSE OF RHYTHM, FOCUS ON THE SPEED AT WHICH YOU ROTATE YOUR UPPER BODY AND **SWEEP** THE BALL CLEANLY OFF THE PEG.

Eyes closed heightens your senses

When you lose one of your senses, others generally sharpen to compensate. Based on that assumption, swinging a club with your eyes closed is another great way to develop your sense of harmony and tempo.

Take your normal set up, and make a number of practice swings with your eyes shut tight. Immediately you will be aware of the way your body works, and receive instant feedback of where exactly your tempo originates. When I do this my senses are drawn towards my shoulders. That's where I feel my swing is controlled. You might find you get a better sense of control from your chest, or your arms. Repeat this exercise for several minutes, until you get a clear picture in your mind's eye of the way everything gels together.

Another important element of the swing you need to be aware of is the *sound* you make. Again, this is heightened when you close your eyes. Make a few practice swings with a 3-wood, and listen to the wind whistle off the shaft. The trick is to keep your body as *quiet* as possible, and build acceleration gradually, so that your maximum force – and the loudest swish – is spent through impact. I play my best golf when I sense that I control the tempo of my swing from *within* my body. I turn my shoulders and feel momentum build gradually, without forcing the issue. Every great player has the ability to generate clubhead speed in this efficient manner.

Swinging in deep rough is another good exercise. I did this a great deal as a junior. Against the resistance of the long grass you have no option but to swing the club back and wind up slowly – it's impossible to snatch the clubhead away. So you build your speed and acceleration gradually, and then rip through the grass. *Your ideal tempo is that which enables you to produce the maximum acceleration at the bottom of your swing.* Try this as a warm-up exercise before you tee off. It really does wake up your golfing muscles.

'Quiet' legs help you unwind your upper body

For overall flow and continuity, nothing is more important than your timing at the start of the downswing. You are aiming for a flawless blending of the two halves that enables your arms and body to unwind in sync, and so generate the most efficient force at impact. A sure way to ruin the fluency of this chain reaction is driving your legs forward as you start down. That was my problem for many years, and as long as I play the game I will always have to watch what my legs are doing. Old habits die hard. Here are a couple of specific exercises I use that help develop a good leg action, and as a result inspire a consistent tempo.

First, hit balls with your feet split apart, as I am doing here. Take your regular set-up position, then simply draw your left foot back until the toe of your shoe is level with your right heel. Any tendency you might have to slide your knees towards the target at the start of the downswing is now history. So placed, your legs can do nothing but support the rotary motion of your body – and that's the key to a repeating swing.

The real beauty of this drill is that it denies you the opportunity to rush the transition, and so you develop a wonderful sense of timing at the top of your swing. Feel the muscles in your torso stretch like strong elastic as you coil your upper body, then let it all unwind. Wait for your moment – instinct will tell you when – and then release the whole of your right side through impact. Tee the ball up and hit as many shots as you like with this drill – it can only do you good.

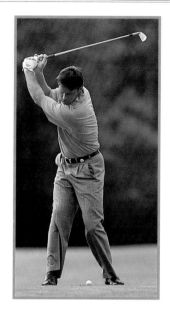

Working on the principle that only a balanced swing will enable you to pick the ball cleanly off sand, it's a good idea also to practise hitting full shots out of a fairway bunker. Don't shuffle your shoes into the sand like you do to play a normal sand shot; imagine you are standing on eggshells as you set up to the ball. The key to this exercise is that you stay *light* on your feet.

Take a mid-iron and challenge the accuracy of your striking. On such a delicate footing the only way you can hope to release the clubhead at a consistent

depth is to pace and control your swing with a passive leg action. Focus on the rotary motion of your upper body, and feel your arms freewheel in response as you unwind to face the target. Lose your rhythm and you lose hope of a good shot.

    Swinging a golf club on the carpet at home wearing street shoes will similarly test the quality of your leg action and general balance. If your swing is too forceful or disjointed, you are likely to slip. Relax, and let the mechanics of your swing unfold in the proper sequence. Feel the weight and momentum of the clubhead on the end of the shaft, and keep your footing secure.

ALTERNATE CLUBS, DISCIPLINE YOUR MIND

I might hit a dozen balls with a 5-iron, but then out of the blue I switch to a driver and hit a couple of shots. I tell myself I still have the 5-iron in my hands, and try to make the same swing, the same effort. I go back to a short iron and continue to hit another dozen shots, always with a target in mind. Then I pull out my 1-iron and make myself believe I'm swinging a wedge. This random chopping and changing between clubs is a sure way to discipline your mind. It breeds a consistent rhythm through your entire game.

Another technique I use from time to time is swinging the club in *ultra* slow motion. If I have been firing shots at a flag with a 7-iron, I drop back to a five, and try to fly the ball 7-iron distance. Forced to swing the club with about 50 per cent of my normal effort, I can feel the way my body works and iron out any kinks that go undetected at regular speed.

Any time I mention this drill I am reminded of a wonderful story concerning the great Irish player Christy O'Connor. Practising for the Open at Troon in 1973, Christy had missed the green at the *Postage Stamp* – the 126-yard eighth hole. Someone in the gallery brought it upon himself to remind Christy that he had just missed one of the shortest holes in championship golf with a 9-iron. Christy emptied out a dozen balls, and with a masterly rhythm and grace he proceeded to hit the green with *every* club in his bag – including his driver.

There's another benefit to be had swinging in slow motion. The easier you swing the club, the less backspin you impact on the ball and the lower it flies towards the target. Out of this discovery we can isolate one of the most valuable lessons in game strategy and ball control. If you work on the principle of always clubbing up on the course, you will find your target more often. Where you would normally take a 5-iron, play your four, and so on. Not only will this encourage you to swing *within* your ability, it will yield a more attacking brand of golf. You won't be the player always short of the green; your ball will finish at least pin high.

Postage Stamp – Troon 8th

THROUGH THE BAG –
one swing fits all

A lot of people ask me how they should adjust their swing to accommodate the different lofts and lie angles between clubs, but this is not something you should worry about. Learning one swing is hard enough, so don't complicate matters. Your only concern should be with setting up to the ball correctly, based on the fundamental lessons we discussed in Chapter 2, and then on turning your upper body back and through towards the target.

My swing thoughts are the same whether I'm using a 3- or a 9-iron. As the length of the shaft increases, I simply adjust my posture accordingly, and the plane of my swing automatically flattens out. The key is to make as full a shoulder turn as you can, and synchronize all the moving parts in your swing. With the longer irons and woods, as the length of the shaft increases, you should feel that your shoulders turn progressively further than your hips – therein lies the secret of a good coil.

Check your swing regularly in front of a mirror. A useful tip is simply to turn your left shoulder under your chin so that your back faces the target. Let physics take care of the details. The length of your arc will naturally increase as you move up through the longer irons and woods, and as momentum builds so your clubhead speed is progressively greater through the ball.

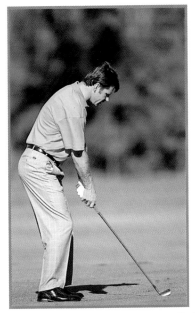
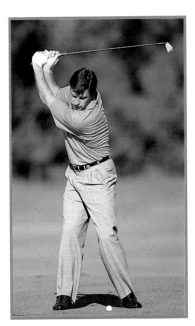

3-iron

9-iron

TROUBLESHOOTING –
isolate key areas in your swing

Nine times out of ten, if I lose my rhythm out on the course it's because I get too quick, or jerky, either at the takeaway or from the top of the swing. Those are the two most vulnerable areas that you have to be aware of. If you snatch the club away from the ball, your swing is immediately out of sync. Similarly, if you rush your downswing without really completing your backswing, you stand to lose 'linkage' and continuity.

A poor takeaway can often be traced to poor posture, for instance your back is too rounded or your shoulders are slumped. As soon as that happens your hands and arms will tend to move away from the ball independently of your body. Your posture simply does not encourage good linkage in the swing, and so your movements become disjointed.

Remember, the first two or three feet of your backswing must be made quite slowly and deliberately. Only then can you build up your speed gradually and forge a fluent chain reaction. So at the first sign of trouble, focus on the fundamental principles of the set up then concentrate on making a good takeaway. Remember your swing trigger, or *pressure release*. Something has to move to make your swing happen. Have a waggle, move your hips or press with your knee – anything that triggers a smooth and synchronized movement away from the ball.

One of the toughest lessons in golf is that you can get lazy with your set-up and posture even when you are hitting the ball well. I've talked to many great players on this matter, and experience has taught them all the same thing. *You have to be ruthless in terms of your pre-shot routine.* That word *routine* has cropped up before, and you must not underestimate its importance. Your pre-shot routine is your key to consistency and certainly your key to withstanding pressure, as and when you face it. The players who are successful on tour are the players who are ruthless every time they set up to the ball, and ruthless in their general self-discipline.

DRILL

Hitting from the top

Hitting from the top is a fault that troubles a great many amateur players, and to a lesser degree it can also upset the professional. Of course, it goes against all I have said about progressively winding and unwinding the swing, and does nothing to enhance your grace or tempo. If you unwind too early, you get 'snatchy' at the top, which can lead to all sorts of problems through the ball. So how do you re-establish a good transition and get your downswing back on track?

You have a number of options. Take your driver, turn it around so that you grip the head, and swing the shaft. You won't make a positive 'swish' through impact until you unwind properly and build acceleration gradually, so regard this as a test. Make a full wind up and full stretch, but swing slowly – feel your tempo come from within your body – and make the wind whistle. I do this often on the course during a tournament.

Another exercise you might see me do from time to time is splitting my hands apart on the grip, and making a slow motion swing. The benefits of doing this are twofold. First, it encourages my arms and body to work together at the start of the swing, so it helps my takeaway. Second, it inspires good width at the top of the swing, and this is maintained at the start of the downswing. So you kill two birds with one stone.

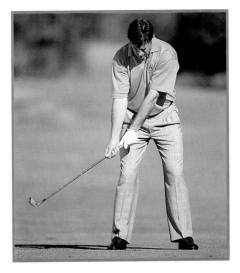

BEATING 100 BALLS
WITH A DRIVER
DOESN'T FORM THE
BASIS OF A GOOD
WARM-UP SESSION.
SWITCH BETWEEN
CLUBS AND WORK ON
MAINTAINING A GOOD
RHYTHM WITH THEM
ALL. WORK UP AND
DOWN THE SCALE.

TAKING YOUR GAME TO THE COURSE

Working on the practice ground, hitting ball after ball, you naturally get better, but you also tend to get quicker and quicker. In so-called 'muscle memory' mode you are likely to rip every shot at your target. Then you have a drink and go to the first tee five minutes later, and it's impossible to reproduce that last swing.

So how do you take that tempo from the practice range to the course? Let me explain how I make that transition with a typical tournament warm-up routine.

The first thing I do on the practice tee is run through a checklist of the fundamentals – grip, alignment, posture and so on. As much as I play, it might

seem unlikely that I ever find much wrong with my set-up, but you can't afford to take any risks. Small faults here multiply over time, and lead to much bigger faults in your swing.

Once I'm happy with my set-up position, I stretch the muscles in my body with a regular pivot exercise, then ease myself into the session with a wedge or 9-iron. All I'm interested in is getting a feel for my swing; being the shortest and easiest clubs to hit, they also bolster my confidence. I don't worry too much about aiming at a target to begin with. These are purely 'looseners'.

After a few minutes I work up through the irons – one day the odd numbers, the next day the evens – and hit four or five balls with each club. With my swing now in full flow, I hit at the most half a dozen balls with the long irons and woods, then drop back to a pitching wedge and begin the process of winding down. This is important. You need what I call a 'cooling off' period, time to calm your muscles before you head for the golf course.

After hitting balls for twenty minutes, I turn my attention to the short game. I play a handful of bunker shots to get a feel for the sand, then stroke one or two chip shots to establish the speed of the greens. Finally, and with the countdown now ten minutes to tee-off, I spend ten minutes with the putter, knocking in short putts and rolling the ball from 20 or 30 feet. Ten minutes putting is ample. Now I'm ready to play.

For me, such a routine takes forty minutes. Assuming things are running to schedule, I step from the putting green to the first tee, and prepare for the game. Should there be a delay, I keep myself occupied. I might reach for a mid-iron and make a few easy swings beside the tee – that keeps my muscles warm. On another day, I might take out a wedge. With the short shaft, my wedge swing helps me capture the tempo and rhythm of a good swing. I can feel my body swinging the club, as opposed to the club swinging my body, which tends to be the case with the longer shafted driver. Even better if there is a patch of rough near by. Then I can swing the clubhead and feel the resistance of the grass.

All this preparation is geared towards striking the first shot of the day, which in my book is probably the most important. It sets the tone for your whole round. Split the fairway with a solid drive and you stride off full of confidence. But if you knock the ball into trouble you immediately feel deflated. So don't automatically reach for your driver. Take the club you feel most confident with. A 3-wood is often a better bet. The extra loft helps to put your mind at ease, and so you are more likely to hit a good shot. I focus on one key thought – usually something to do with tempo – then take a couple of deep breaths and make my swing.

Another thought I find to be extremely useful on the first tee, and this is specifically geared towards good tempo, is that of *collecting* the ball through impact. Stand there and tell yourself that the ball gets in the way of a good swing. Don't try to hit the ball too hard, simply turn back and through and put the ball in play. That's your priority.

One last point. If a good warm-up routine takes forty minutes, allow yourself at least forty minutes before you tee off. If you rush to the course, fall out of your car and on to the tee, you deserve to play badly.

THE FAIRWAY WOOD –
same unhurried swing, same unhurried rhythm

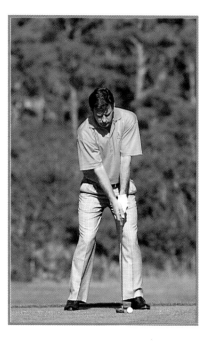

Knees

Rotate and set

Turn

COMPARE THESE IMAGES OF A 3-WOOD SEQUENCE WITH THE 5-IRON I WAS USING IN CHAPTER 1. IN THIS CASE, THE CLUB IS SLIGHTLY LONGER. THE BALL IS FRACTIONALLY FURTHER AWAY FROM MY BODY, AND THE ARC OF MY SWING IS NATURALLY GREATER. BUT THE RHYTHM REMAINS THE SAME, AND MY **KEY THOUGHTS** AGAIN HELP ME TO PRODUCE A REPEATING SWING AND **SWEEP** THE BALL CLEANLY OFF THE FAIRWAY.

Slow and unwind   Watch it   Low hands

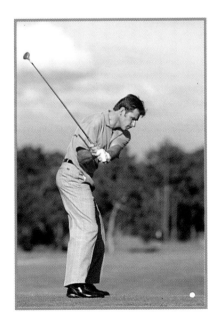

5
WORKING THE BALL

*Shaping shots is the senior-school element in your
education as a golfer. The ability to work the ball at will
is the key to plotting and coping with the special demands of the wind.*

Playing in the San Diego Open at Torrey Pines in 1982, I found myself in the company of a rampant Jack Nicklaus and big-hitting Andy Bean. Between them they ripped the course apart. Nicklaus returned a glorious 64, Bean took 68. I shot a lacklustre 71, which at the time felt more like 81.

Later that afternoon I found myself analyzing Jack's round. I had been treated to a rare display of perfect ball-striking. Wherever the pin was placed, Jack's iron shots tore off for the middle of the green before leaning one way or the other to seek out the flag, as if they were guided by radar. If the pin was cut to the right, his shots fell obediently to the right. If the pin was tucked to the left, his shots tapered left.

This was Nicklaus doing what Nicklaus did best – *thinking* his way around a course and *working* the ball to order. He never looked like missing a green. On the odd occasion he caught one of his iron shots 'flush', he would finish up in the heart of the green, leaving a 20-foot birdie putt instead of the usual 5-footer. 64 was the worst score he could do that day.

Looking back on my career, that experience had a profound effect on my decision to change my swing. I wanted to be one of the best players in the world, and to achieve that goal I needed the versatility to work the ball both ways. It's a skill that anyone with ambition to play at the highest level must develop.

SHAPE YOUR SHOTS –
increase your margin for error

Many people have accused me of being a 'mechanical' player, but how little they know. Within the framework of a sound and reliable body movement, my entire game is based on my ability to manipulate the trajectory of my shots with a subtle hand and arm action through impact. That's not mechanical – that's instinctive golf.

It hardly needs to be said that spinning the ball is an advanced technique. But when you get to the stage where your swing is in sync – when your arm swing complements a good body movement as we discussed in Chapter 3 – you can begin to think about the nature of impact and experiment with the way you release the clubhead. Leave this section well alone until then.

Every player has a natural shape of shot, either a fade or a draw, and that must form the basis of your strategy from tee to green. Always play to your strengths. The best management advice anyone can give you is visualize and play the shot you have the greatest chance of pulling off. If you apply that logical chain of thinking to your next game you will make an instant saving.

My own preference is the fade, a gentle curve from left to right that might deviate by only 10 or 15 feet in the air. As that's the shape I feel most comfortable playing, wherever possible that's the shot I go looking for out on the course. But your natural spin does not always fit the bill. As your game develops you will start to think more in terms of attacking the pin – not just hitting the green – and then you discover the real challenge of working the ball. You need the ability to shape your shots in either direction, so every pin is accessible.

If the pin is cut towards the back left-hand corner of the green, my instinct is to fire a shot for the middle of the green with draw. On the other hand, if I face a shot to a flag cut tight behind a bunker in the front right quarter of the green, I play a fade. In both cases I aim for the fat of the green, and let the ball work towards the pin. That's the key. Just as Nicklaus proved to me all those years ago, the smart shot is the one that errs on the side of caution.

In any sort of a wind, the plot thickens.

Let's suppose a shot of 160 yards – something in the order of a 5- or 6-iron. There's a breeze blowing from the right and the pin is cut tight on the right side of the green. The only way to land and stop the ball close to the hole is to neutralize the effect of the wind with counter spin – in this case a fade. Aiming dead on the flag, I would try to make a punchy, three-quarter swing, and pull the clubface across the ball to fashion a shot that holds its line with a subtle left-to-right spin. A difficult shot, certainly, but one the accomplished golfer must develop.

Stuck in a similar situation, the one-way right-to-left player finds himself in trouble. He is forced to aim away to the right of the target in the hope that the wind will bring the ball back. He has no real control. As the ball reaches the apex of its flight and turns towards the pin, it is actually sailing downwind and so is unlikely to settle quickly on the green.

Clearly, having the ability to feel the clubhead, and work the ball with spin – both left and right – opens up a whole new dimension to your game. In many cases, gently curving the ball through the air also widens your margin for error. Think about your strategy off the tee. If your normal shape is a fade, the best policy is to aim down the left side of the fairway and let the ball work its way back towards the middle. That way you effectively increase your landing area.

My Ryder Cup partner Colin Montgomerie sets a good example. A natural left-to-right player, Colin feeds the ball down the left side and watches it drift back into the heart of the fairway. And he hits more fairways than most. Ian Woosnam works on the same principle, but his game is based on a right-to-left draw. You will find more advice on your strategy off the tee in Chapter 6.

To take a different angle, working the ball can also be your best line of defence under pressure. I often find myself in a position where I cannot afford to let the ball leak to the right or left, and so my thoughts are geared towards blocking out one side of the course. Take the second shot on the eleventh hole at Augusta – the gateway to Amen Corner. Assuming a good drive, I am usually left facing a shot of between 170 and 190 yards, and with water lurking on the left side of the green – and plenty room to the right – the last thing I want to do is hit the ball with right-to-left spin. My approach to playing this hole is always to go in with a fade, a shot that does all it can to work away from the hazard.

Let me demonstrate some of the specialist techniques that I use to work the ball, and offer some suggestions that might spice up your practice time and expand your repertoire of shots out on the course.

EXPERIENCE WILL TEACH YOU TO **FEEL** THE SHAPE OF A SHOT – RESTRICTING THE RELEASE FOR A FADE (*OPPOSITE*), AND ROTATING BOTH THE CLUB AND YOUR BODY HARD THROUGH THE BALL FOR A DRAW (*BELOW*).

ADVANCED TECHNIQUE

THE FADE – 'hold off' the clubface

The majority of the shots I play are created with 'feel'. It makes no odds whether I need a fade or a draw. Working around a consistent set-up position, I simply picture the shape in my mind and feel the desired spin in my hands and arms as I swing the clubhead through impact.

Manufacturing shots in this way relies entirely on the quality of your feel and natural ball skills. From midway in the downswing to the corresponding point in the follow through, you conjure up the necessary formula to make the ball spin, feeling the shot in your hands and forearms. As I've said, my own natural shape is a fade, a safe shot that might only curve a few feet in the air. If I need to accentuate that left-to-right spin, say I need to protect the line of a shot against a stronger wind, I employ a technique known as 'holding off' the clubface through impact. In other words, I do all I can to prevent the toe of the clubface turning over the heel, as it would do normally. When I set up to play this type of shot, my thoughts are focused on making my backswing in the usual manner, then on clearing my side fairly aggressively and holding the position of my left arm steady through impact. This subtle action of cutting across the ball is all that is needed to induce a hint of left-to-right spin and so urge the ball to fly and hold its line with a fade.

REMEMBER, YOU WILL TEND TO LOSE A LITTLE DISTANCE WITH THE LEFT TO RIGHT SHAPE, SO AS YOU VISUALIZE THE SHOT IN YOUR MIND ALWAYS CLUB UP.

Such intuitive shot-making takes time and patience to master, but go out and see what you can do. Rotate your left forearm and set your wrists to make your backswing, then hold the position of your left arm and the clubface firm through impact. The sensation you are looking for is that of your hips and shoulders turning and working faster than the clubhead through impact, so your arms follow suit and pull the club across the ball. I sometimes imagine there's a small piece of sandpaper on the clubface, and rip it hard across the cover.

Another useful tip here is to grip the club a little more firmly with your left hand. That makes good sense any time you set up to play a left-to-right shot, as it encourages a firm left wrist through impact.

Characteristic of this technique is the distinctive follow-through position, specifically that of the left arm. I call it the 'wing'. See how my left elbow works out and up as my hands and arms lead the clubhead through impact. Depending on how severely I hold off the release in this fashion, I can move the ball up to 20 feet through the air, or half the width of a green.

I used the wing to pull off one of the most important shots in my life during the Open at Muirfield in 1992. A good drive had left me 165 yards from the pin at the fifteenth hole, and against a gusting wind I squeezed in a low 5-iron, aiming to land the ball 15 feet left of the flag. It worked out perfectly. The ball fought tooth and nail to hold its line, landed on exactly the spot I had chosen and followed the contours of the green to finish 5 feet from the flag.

ADVANCED TECHNIQUE

THE DRAW – *think 'rotate and release'*

Without making any conscious adjustment to my set-up position, I again manufacture the release with my hands and forearms to play a draw, a gentle shot that curves from right to left through the air. I work on rotating my left forearm away from the ball just as normal to make my backswing, but this time focus on re-rotating my left arm through impact, so the clubface turns over the ball and imparts right-to-left spin.

It all sounds very complicated, but if you study this sequence and compare it with similar images of the fade, the differences will be clear. To induce that right-to-left spin, you must encourage your right forearm to cross over the left with a more rounded angle of attack. Feel it as you release your hands and arms. You want the toe end of the club to turn over the heel, so the clubface wraps itself around the ball.

Let me simplify this further with a visual swing key that I use out on the course. Imagine the clubface is a gate. Your job is to open and close the gate during the swing. When you set up to play the draw, work on rotating your left forearm away from the ball in the backswing to open the clubface (the gate), then re-rotate your left forearm and close the gate through impact.

THE ROTARY ACTION OF MY BODY SETS THE RHYTHM OF THE SWING, WHILE MY HANDS AND ARMS COME ALIVE TO FEEL AND MANIPULATE THE ANGLE OF THE CLUBFACE THROUGH IMPACT.

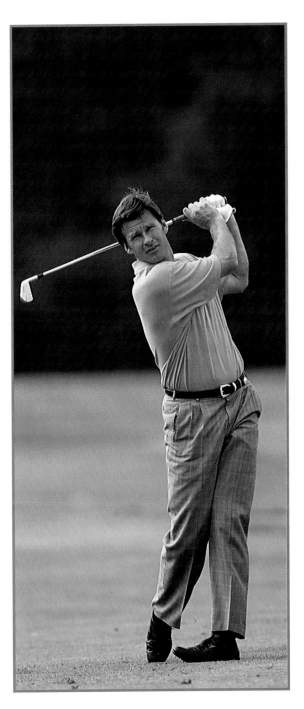

Every picture tells a story. Playing the fade, the restricted, slightly held-off finish matches perfectly my intention to cut across the ball and spin it from left to right. By comparison, the fuller and flatter 'wrap-around' position you see here is the natural conclusion to rolling the clubface over the ball when the emphasis is on spinning a shot from right to left.

For many players, this body language is the key to shaping shots, and certainly you need to be aware of the special relationships involved between the nature of the follow-through position and your intention to manufacture different shots.

Another way to grasp the principle of spinning the ball is to visualize a tennis player hitting a similar shot. Take the fade. Imagine the clubhead is a large tennis racket, and picture yourself 'holding off' and pulling the strings across the ball to create the left-

to-right spin. Feel the release as you conjure up a sort of defensive floating shot.

The draw is a more aggressive top-spin drive. Let the racket turn over the ball, and feel the way your right forearm works over the left through impact. Use this type of mental imagery to simplify your concept of the ball-flight laws, and boost your versatility and your confidence on the practice tee.

A SIMPLER TECHNIQUE –
How to create spin with your set-up position

I split working the ball into two categories. On the one hand I use spin to neutralize the effect of the wind, or to shape a shot off the tee. This is the *feel* in me that might only move the ball a few feet when my strategy calls for smart attacking golf.

But you do not always have the luxury of choice, and working the ball around trouble is the other key element of this chapter. That your education as a golfer be complete, you need the ability to bend shots to negotiate your way around trees, hillocks and other obstacles. The basic technique I recommend you adopt to play an intentional fade or draw – the one I first learned as a junior – is very simple: everything revolves around your alignment.

Working from left to right

Let's start with the fade. To make the ball spin from left to right, aim the leading edge of the clubface at the point where you want the ball to finish, then adjust your body alignment until your hips, knees and shoulders are open in

relation to your target. Position the ball in the forward part of your stance, and spread your weight evenly between your feet.

Now for the simple part: *once you have built in the necessary adjustments you are free to make your regular swing.* It's like playing golf on one of those computer games. You first select the appropriate alignment of the clubface, then offset the alignment of your body before firing the button. With the clubface and the line of your swing effectively at odds, you have now *pre-set* the formula required to make the ball spin. Here, with a 5-iron, the ball will initially fly on the line of my body, then turn and soar to the right. If I needed to accentuate the curve, I would open up my stance even further – the 'spin factor' is thus increased – and my swing would be programmed to cut more severely across the ball. As and when I deem it to be necessary I might also add to the sliding effect with a conscious effort to *hold off* the clubface through impact.

You will find when you practise these shots that it is very difficult to make the ball curve hard with anything shorter than a 7-iron. The more loft on the clubface, the more backspin you tend to create, which overrides any sidespin. Keep that in mind.

Working the ball from right to left

Make the opposite adjustments in your set up to play a right-to-left draw. Aim the clubface on your target, but this time settle your body in a closed position, the line across your shoulders reflecting the direction in which you want the ball to start. Now, geared up to swing along a more circular path, your key thought this time is to rotate the clubface through impact. Try to make the toe-end of the club turn over the heel, and 'close the gate' on the ball. Commit yourself to releasing the right side of your body and chase the ball with your right shoulder to a relatively flat finish. Your hands should arrive at a low, comfortable position behind your neck.

The mechanics involved in playing a draw will naturally de-loft the clubface, so expect the ball to fly a little lower than normal and allow for extra run. Take one less club and aim for the front of the green.

Curving the ball from right to left is generally the easier of the two shots for the right-handed player, and as you become more confident you can stretch this 'offset' principle to its limits to play a low raking hook. In this example I have doctored my set-up to turn the ball around the far tree at the corner of the dog-

leg. The clubface is aimed where I want the ball to finish, but my body is positioned something in the order of 40 degrees closed in relation to that line. With a naturally rounded swing, my hands are encouraged to be quite active through impact, and the crossover slings the ball out to the right with so much spin that it bends like a banana.

The only way to feel comfortable shaping your shots out on the course is to go away and practise. If there is somewhere you can hit balls with a tree as an obstacle, all the better. Take a mid-iron and bend a few shots around the branches with a fade. Then go the other way. Challenge your versatility, and sling the ball around the corner with a right-to-left spin. Such trial and error is good for your game generally, and quickly enhances your feel for the clubhead.

Experiment with the ball position, too, as that can have a dramatic effect on the shape and trajectory of your shots. Play the ball forward in your stance for extra height and spin, then gradually move it back, towards the middle, for a lower, punchier flight.

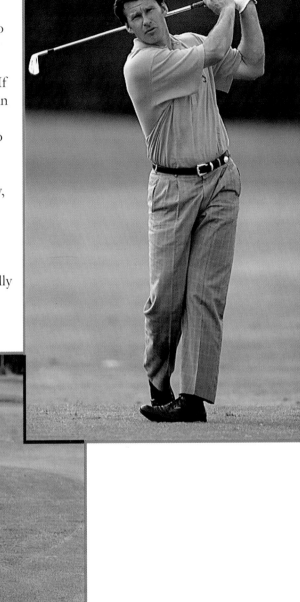

HOIST THE BALL HIGH . . .

Let's turn our attention specifically to what I call the highs and lows of shot-making. Suppose you have a shot of 140 yards, and your line to the pin is blocked by a tall tree. There is no way you can hope to go around the tree *and* hold the green, while the option to play beneath the branches simply does not exist. You have to go over.

Typically, a shot of this distance would call for a 9-iron, but I would take my 8-iron and play the ball well forward in my stance, which, you will notice, is fairly well open in relation to the target. With the emphasis on maximizing *upward* momentum through impact, I then settle the majority of my weight on the right side, and also remind myself to keep a fairly light and relaxed grip pressure. I

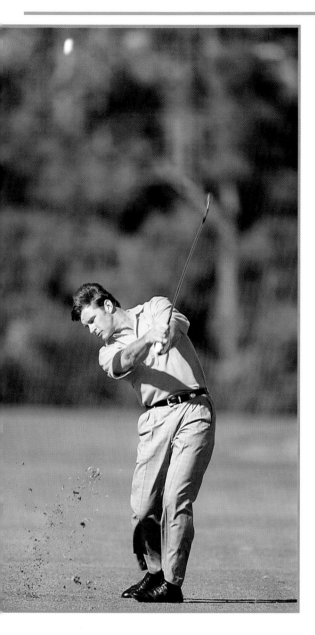
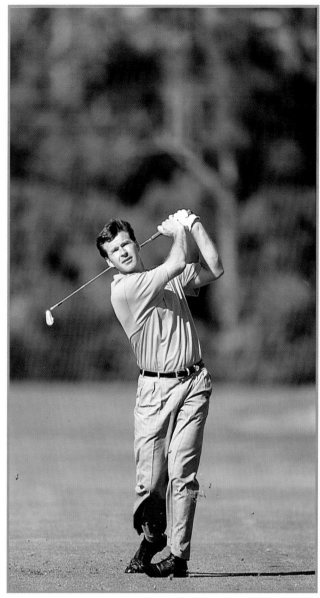

want my hands and arms to be fairly active and accelerate freely through impact, so that grip pressure is important. These adjustments effectively *add* loft to the clubface and give me the feeling of being physically *behind* the shot. Once I am ready to play, I make a full swing and focus on sliding the clubface cleanly beneath the ball. Through impact I am conscious of hoisting the ball high into the air, and the shot flies softly with a touch of left-to-right spin. The high-handed finish that you see here clearly reflects my intention to reach for the sky.

When I practise, I often play games to see just how high I can hit the ball with a whole span of irons. Similarly, it's important that you establish your own 'safe' range. Take a bag of balls and see how close you can get to a tree, yet still fly a shot clean over the top. Work on releasing your hands and wrists until you can feel the ball leave the clubface.

. . . AND PUNCH IT LOW

For many amateurs the low punch shot is the harder of the two extremes. The problem, I think, is that there is a tendency to want to play the ball too far back in the stance, which encourages a steep swing. I see a lot of players reach for a long iron – say a 3- or a 4-iron – then move the ball back to a position opposite the right heel *and* push their hands forward. That 3-iron is now looking more like a 1-iron. Even before they attempt to play the shot they have smothered the ball.

So make club selection your first consideration. No matter how dramatic the situation, I rarely take anything less than a 4- or 5-iron, because by the time I have finalized my set up, with the ball in the middle of my stance and my hands eased gently forward, the natural loft is greatly reduced. To enhance feel and control over the shot, I usually choke down a little on the grip. And my weight favours my left side throughout.

Once I am comfortable at address, I focus on rotating my left forearm away from the ball and setting my wrists to make my backswing, just as normal. That

prevents my swing getting too steep. Then, with the emphasis on maintaining a good rhythm as I change direction, I commit myself to pulling *down and through*, with my left side firm as my body turns to face the target and my arms swing the clubhead into the back of the ball.

Any time your priority is punching low ball, the key is to make your body release *ahead* of the clubhead. It's a bit like hitting a cover drive in cricket. As long as your body turns out of the way, and your hands and arms lead the club-face through impact, the natural loft is denied and the ball is 'knocked down'. The relatively low and restricted follow-through is further evidence of your intention to 'bunt' the ball forwards.

Take your 5-iron and experiment moving the ball between the middle and the rear part of your stance. Preset the impact position you want to achieve, then throttle back and make a three-quarter swing. Don't ever try to hit these shots too hard, either. Try to be as *quiet* as you can through the ball. If you get too aggressive you are likely to create backspin, which defeats the object.

THE RELATIVELY LOW, RESTRICTED FOLLOW-THROUGH SAYS IT ALL. COMPARE THIS TO THE FULLY RELEASED POSITION I ACHIEVE PLAYING THE HIGH SHOT. REMEMBER, YOUR BODY ACTION CONTROLS THE SHAPE AND TRAJECTORY OF ALL YOUR SHOTS.

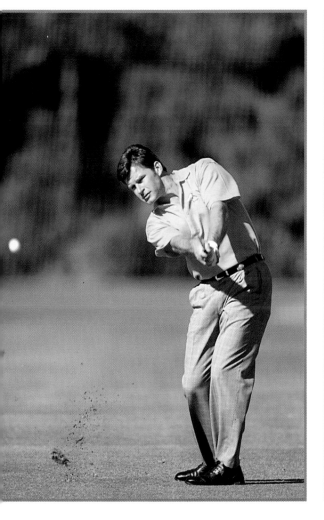

HOW TO CONTROL YOUR GAME IN THE WIND

I have always enjoyed traditional links golf. I relish the challenge of controlling the ball in an ever-changeable fresh sea breeze. I regard that as being the true test of clubhead control and strategy.

I hit my 7-iron about 155 yards in calm conditions. On a links, against a moderate headwind, I might need a 5-iron to achieve that same distance. The effect the wind has on the length and trajectory of your shots never ceases to amaze me – your yardages do become almost irrelevant.

The key to controlling your game in the wind is first to swallow your pride and discipline your mind. You have to accept the conditions as they are. Be realistic. If the regular par of the course is 72, and you normally shoot in the mid-80s, your 'personal par' on a gusty day could be closer to 90. If you adjust your sights in this way, not only will you enjoy your game a whole lot more, you will probably score better, too. Remember, the wind doesn't just blow for you.

As far as a shot-making strategy is concerned, *my first rule against any sort of breeze is to club up and swing easy,* and you should make it yours. I talked about this briefly in Chapter 4, and the 'less is more' approach really is the key to solid ball-striking from tee to green. When you swing the club smoothly you strike the ball more solidly and your shots fly with a lower and more penetrating trajectory, so you minimize the buffeting effects of the wind.

Guard against any tendency to quicken your swing in the wind. Your natural composure is vulnerable on a blustery day, so try to think in terms of maintaining a good rhythm and balance. I usually focus on holding my follow-through position rock solid – right through the bag, from driver to putter – and that breeds a solid action through the ball. I stress, good balance is vital.

Be aggressive around the green too. A headwind multiplies any backspin and makes the ball stop more quickly than normal, so aim for the top of the flag on your pitch shots, and be bold on the runners.

Though it is not as threatening as a headwind, think clearly about your strategy when a tail wind pushes you along. Your tee shots stand to benefit the most. A high 3-wood will often sail as far – *if not further* – than a well-struck driver. The ball hangs in the air longer.

Remember, *downward you have to consider trouble that ordinarily would be out of reach.* Particularly on a links course, hazards that may be 250 or 300 yards away are feasibly in range.

In a severe wind, I will often opt for the safety of a 3- or 4-iron, and use the yardage book to establish a safe landing distance. You must always think one step ahead. Playing a moderate length par-4, you don't want to get too close to the green. The 1st hole at St Andrews is a great example of this strategy. Although the fairway is about as generous as you will ever find in championship golf, most players prefer to take an iron club off the tee so as to leave themselves with a full shot over the burn.

A tail wind also makes it difficult to hold the ball on a green. No matter how much backspin you think you put on the ball, the wind will deny it, so aim to land on the front edge, or even short of the green. Work with the subtle banks and borrows that exist and *feed* the ball towards the hole. There are no set rules, particularly where a links course is involved, so widen your target area. On a normal day I expect to pitch the ball to within a 20 foot circle, but when the wind blows hard I might double that.

Working the ball in a crosswind is a skill you can only develop with practice. Don't expect too much too soon. Shaping the trajectory of your shots with intentional spin is an advanced technique, and until you are capable of such control you must allow for the wind.

Off the tee or on the fairway, when a crosswind threatens, the key is to aim off to the left or right, and focus on a specific target. Pick out a distinct landmark on the horizon and commit yourself to swinging and releasing the club *on that line*. Your job is to hit a straight shot – let the wind do the rest. And remember, any ball that rides the wind flies *farther* and runs a little more willingly than it would do normally. So think hard before you pull a club out of your bag.

6
MY DRIVING STRATEGY

We all live in the hope of adding a few extra yards off the tee,
but the priority is positioning your ball in the fairway.

A couple of years ago I had the privilege of a meeting with golf's most legendary figure, Ben Hogan, at Shady Oaks, his club in Texas. His shared thoughts on every single aspect of the game, and no-nonsense philosophy on driving the ball, make for the perfect introduction to this chapter.

For Hogan, the key to good golf was placing the tee-ball on a chosen spot in the fairway. A drive was not measured in yards, but analyzed in terms of position. If a hole featured a dog-leg and the left side of the fairway offered the best angle for a look at the flag, that's where he expected his ball to finish. Every shot was a personal challenge.

Length off the tee was sometimes a factor, but rarely the issue. Like every great player, Hogan knew how and when to turn on the power. Faced with a long par-4 or a reachable 5, the potential rewards warranted the inevitable risk. Otherwise, it was much better to play the percentage game, and make certain of finding the short grass.

These strands of common sense add up to a lesson in course management that should form the foundation of your driving strategy. Hogan had identified for me one of the keys to low scoring: *think not in terms of how far but how accurately you place your ball in the fairway.* That's not defensive golf, it's smart golf.

PLAYING THE YARDAGE GAME

One thing professionals do well that amateurs seldom do at all is study the yardage book to identify the ideal route to the green on every hole. I shall elaborate on this in Chapter 10, but your strategy off the tee is perhaps *the* most important aspect of your game plan.

Firstly, plot a realistic map of the course you play. Look at all the par-4 holes and identify the trouble spots and safety zones. If there are bunkers out there, would a regular drive reach them and should you perhaps be taking a 3-wood to lay-up in the fairway? If there is a boundary fence, or some other hazard lying in wait, you may even consider playing a long iron. Use a marker pen and draw in the ideal line.

Think about what Hogan said. Which side of the hole presents you with the easiest shot at the green? Single out the long 4s and 5s and establish whether or not it is really worth going for the big shot. I would hesitate busting a driver if the only benefit were a 6-iron second, rather than a 5. What difference does one club make? As soon as you force your swing you increase your chances of being wayward with it, and if you end up in the rough you surrender control.

It's not clever to be the guy who comes in and asks everyone what they hit to the long thirteenth, then says he hit one less. You've got a bag of irons to play with, so let them work for you.

On the other hand, if you think you have a chance of reaching a par-5 in two, and there's not too much trouble about, it's worth having a go. The fifteenth hole at Augusta is a good example. I always try to launch a big drive at this 500-yard hole, because if I get hold of one I can reach the green with an iron. Even if I don't catch it flush I know I can lay-up for a possible pitch-and-putt birdie. So, it's a no-lose gamble.

The fifteenth hole at Harbor Town is a classic three-shotter that makes for an interesting comparison. Ranked as one of the toughest par-5s in America, you can hit a driver, but there's no point. A narrow path lined with tall trees allows no leeway on the drive. The fairway does not open up at the landing area, and the green is out of reach in two shots. You are forced to play a 'tactical lay-up'. My game plan is always to take a 3-wood or a 1-iron off the tee, depending on the wind, and then aim to land a mid-iron on the right side of the fairway for a good look at the green with my third.

The wind is another factor you have to consider, in tandem with potential hazards and the shape of the hole. If the wind is blowing off the left and the trouble is all down that side, then you are in luck. Using the wind as a safety blanket you can aim left and watch your ball drift into the fairway. But if the wind is blowing from right-to-left, and water flanks the left side, you have to work a little harder. I would always try to spin the ball *against* the wind as far as possible and play a gentle fade, aiming at the spot I want the ball to finish. It all boils down to how confident you are. In a stronger wind – over 10 or 15 miles an hour – you have to rethink your strategy. It's tough to fight such a wind, so allow for it.

All this is skill you learn with experience. But you should never underestimate the effect of the wind. Any time it's blowing across or from behind, double-check your yardages and consider trouble that ordinarily would be out of reach. By the time you've shaped your shot the ball might be sailing with the wind, and could easily fly 30 or 40 yards further than normal. A 3-wood will often travel further than a driver. Remember also that when you are playing into the wind, any spin you create will be accentuated many times over. A gentle fade turns into an ugly slice; a controlled draw becomes a hook. So in the wind, remember: *swing easy, minimize spin, and fly the ball low.*

Now that we have covered the safety procedures, let's turn our attention to the swing itself, and consider what it takes to generate clubhead speed and drive the ball a long way.

DON'T BE A SLAVE TO DISTANCE. PLOT YOUR STRATEGY, KEEP THE BALL ON THE SHORT GRASS, AND YOU'LL BE A MATCH FOR ANYONE.

THE DRIVER SWING – *a matter of timing*

It was Sam Snead who said he liked to feel 'as loose as a goose', and Sam had one of the prettiest and most powerful swings the game has ever seen. 'Slammin' Sam' would lighten his grip and let rip through the ball. Like every successful athlete, he knew how to get the most out of his body. Ernie Els reminds me of Snead. He has that nonchalant but perfectly synchronized swing that seems to put the ball into orbit. That's the gift of perfect timing. He can fly it 270 yards without any problem at all. Then, out of the blue, he can add that extra something and drive the ball 300 yards.

Ian Woosnam is another with the ability to create fantastic power with seemingly little effort. He maximizes centrifugal force with a strong shoulder turn, and cracks the ball as if he were cracking a whip. Someone once summed up his swing as 'two turns and a swish', and that's a useful phrase to keep in your mind when you go to work on your long game.

MIND OVER MATTER: IT MAKES NO ODDS HOW BIG AND STRONG YOU ARE, PHYSICAL ABILITY ISN'T WORTH A BEAN IF YOU DON'T KNOW HOW TO USE IT PROPERLY.

One of the easiest and most effective ways to strengthen your body action is to hold a driver out at around waist-height and swish the clubhead baseball style. Feel your shoulders turn fully back and through, and stir up a storm. Make the wind whistle through impact, then re-create that sound with your regular swing. The beauty of this exercise is that it teaches you the discipline of building acceleration gradually, and that's the key to maximizing clubhead speed.

All the great drivers of the ball give themselves the time to maximize the coiling effect in the body with an easy, unhurried rhythm. Jack Nicklaus always said that whenever he needed to cut loose a big drive he actually felt like he made a *slower* move away from the ball. What he meant was he wanted to be sure of giving the muscles in his body time to work properly. I like Jack's way of thinking. When I go in search of distance on the practice tee, one of my key thoughts is 'slow and unwind'. That helps me keep my rhythm. I don't try to swing the club any harder, just *better*.

STRETCHING –
the concept of 'coil' and 'release'

One of the most significant lessons for me in recent years has revolved around this concept of creating and holding resistance in the swing. Like winding a spring, you use your body to build up centrifugal force which is then multiplied through the arms and the clubshaft to create clubhead speed.

With a driver in my hands I like to feel that I stretch the bigger muscles in my upper body, while my knees and hips do all they can to *resist* the rotary motion of my trunk. That gets me fully coiled, or 'loaded'. The first move back

to the ball – often called the 'power move' – is then very much a chain reaction. My weight flows across to my left side almost before my arms have completed the backswing, and throwing the gears into reverse activates the proper down-swing sequence. I think in terms of the shoulders leading the way. In the back-swing, my left shoulder pulls on my left hip and left knee – that gets me fully wound up. Then, once my weight has settled in the transition period, my left shoulder *re-rotates* towards the target, which in turn pulls on the left hip. As my left side clears out of the way I am then free to release the whole right side of my body through the ball.

Turn against a flexed right knee

If a good body action is the engine that drives your swing along, then fine-tuning the mechanics involved is the key to increasing clubhead speed and therefore distance. It's all about forces working against one another. One of the thoughts I have focused on in recent years is turning and coiling my upper body against a flexed and braced right knee. Take a driver and rehearse this slowly in front of a mirror. Work on turning your left shoulder across to a position above your right

knee – get your upper body behind the ball – but keep that right knee and thigh braced. Can you feel the big muscles in your torso stretch as you reach the top of your backswing?

Theory has it you should turn your shoulders through 90 degrees, your hips through 45. I prefer to work on a ratio of 90-degree shoulder turn to 30-degree hip turn. In practice I sometimes hit shots with my right foot hooked in towards the left. That increases the effective resistance in my right thigh and serves to restrict my hip turn. So it tightens the coil.

Now the power move. To unwind the spring, feel your left shoulder and left knee move *together* and pull away from a resisting right side. I refer to this as the moment of *separation,* and it's crucial in terms of your ability to unwind the coil correctly. When you release the spring with this left-side separation you automatically clear the way for your arms to accelerate the clubhead into the back of the ball. It's a chain reaction. Once your weight flows back to the left side, your right shoulder, right hip and right knee – in that order – can fire and add *thrust* as you continue to rotate your upper body through impact.

If there is one piece of advice you take from this book I hope it is that you work on strengthening your leg action to maximize this principle of coil and release. If your legs are dancing about you have nothing secure to turn and push against. But if you wind and unwind the muscles in your upper body over resisting knees and thighs you will witness acceleration like never before.

It is rare that books and magazines feature a swing sequence from the reverse-angle, but I believe it has great merit. Certainly it conveys the impression of the legs as being the real power base in the swing, which is important. Their job is to stabilize and support the rotary motion of the upper body, and these images will help you to develop a similarly passive leg action, one that facilitates a good repeating swing.

Pay particular attention to the 'power move'. Having turned my upper body and shifted my weight on to my right side in the backswing, it

is that subtle moment of separation as the left knee and left shoulder re-rotate towards the target that sets the downswing sequence in motion. Rhythm is of the essence as my lower body assumes that sit-down, 'squat' look, and my hands and arms drop the club into the classic hitting position. My reward is then the freedom to rotate my body hard through the ball as I release the clubhead towards the target. However you look at it, a good swing always features a proud and balanced follow-through position.

SHALLOW YOUR ATTACK FOR A CLEAN SWEEP

I have never been known as a great driver of the ball, but I'm a lot more consistent now than I was ten years ago. The reason is simple. As I have improved my body action I have naturally shallowed the angle of my swing – by lowering the plane of my downswing relative to that of the backswing. This is the natural consequence of winding and unwinding my body correctly, and it's something I keep a close check on when I work on my game.

You can prove this to yourself. Stand side-on to a full-length mirror, and rehearse the power move. Wind your body up, then *unwind in slow motion*. See how your arms and the club return along your backswing plane for the first 10 or 12 inches of their journey. Then, as you continue to rotate your body to the left the shaft angle gradually shallows as your hands drop the club into the classic hitting position. As long as you continue to unwind your body correctly you are now on track to sweep the ball clean off the peg with a free-flowing uninhibited release.

That angle of attack is the key to distance. With the driver you want to catch the ball in the early stages of *ascent*. The bottom of your arc, or the 'flat-spot' in your swing, is three or four inches ahead of the ball. That enables you to rifle your shots away with a low, penetrating trajectory.

One way to develop this skill is to use your 3-wood and hit shots off a high tee-peg. Play the ball opposite your left instep and settle your weight slightly in favour of your right side. That encourages a powerful turn. Then visualize the clubhead travelling level with the ground through impact. Let the clubhead *collect* the ball,

ONCE YOU GET THE BIG MUSCLES IN YOUR BODY TURNING CORRECTLY, YOU CAN UNWIND HARD AND FOCUS ON SWEEPING THE BALL CLEAN OFF THE PEG.

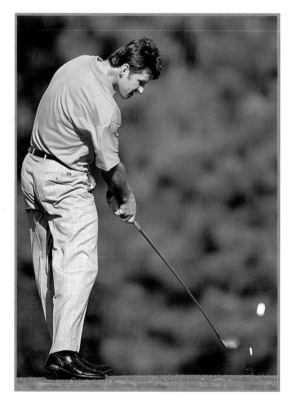

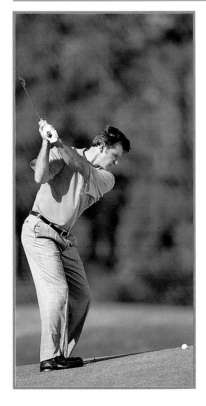

and rip it low through the air. Do this to build confidence at the bottom of your swing, then switch to a driver and go after the same shallow feeling.

Another exercise I recommend to groove a shallow and powerful attack is hitting shots with the ball positioned a few inches above the level of your feet. Use a mid-iron and get used to the sensation of rotary motion as you swing the clubhead in *sympathy* with the slope. In just a few minutes your swing will feel nicely rounded and compact as your shoulders are encouraged to turn back and through on a relatively level plane. Hold your finish in balance, and watch the ball fly with right-to-left spin.

As the quality of your ball-striking improves, work on building up your club-head speed with a driver. Keep a clear image of a player like Ernie Els or Fred Couples lodged in your mind – that will help your rhythm – and channel all your energy towards the all-important moment of impact. Visualize the streaming trajectory of a long drive and make as much noise as you can through the ball.

The ultimate test is hitting a driver off the deck. Experienced players should try this from time to time – it gives you instant feedback on the state of your swing. If you can pick the ball clean off the grass and fire it straight down the fairway, you can feel pretty confident that everything is working in sync. I remember doing this in practice during the Open at Muirfield in 1992, where I enjoyed one of the best ball-striking weeks of my career. All four days of the tournament I finished my warm-up session with a couple of shots off the deck with my driver, and that has become a regular feature of my preparation ever since.

HOW TO CURE THE UGLIEST FAULT IN GOLF

Every swinging motion requires a coordinated body movement and a logical weight shift. By that I mean a player's weight must flow back and forth with the natural progression of the swing.

Think about it. When a tennis player tosses a ball to serve, he winds his body up with his weight on his back foot, then surges forward to initiate the smash. It's the same in golf. Your weight must be encouraged to flow into your right side on the backswing, only to change direction and signal the follow-through.

There are numerous other examples. Whether you are kicking a ball or throwing a punch, your weight must be allowed to move naturally back and forth, and to some degree your head will move as well to provide balance. I let my head ease to the right as I move the club away from the ball, and as a swing trigger that encourages me to shift my weight correctly and load up a powerful coil.

EASING MY HEAD TO THE RIGHT ENABLES MY SPINE TO ROTATE UNRESTRICTED, WHICH MAXIMIZES MY POTENTIAL TO GENERATE POWER AND MINIMIZES THE STRESS ON MY BACK.

Keep your head still – possibly the worst piece of advice anyone can give you, if taken literally. *Keep your head balanced and your eyes on the ball* – I would agree with that. It's important that you watch the ball and maintain a good horizontal level, but *don't make a conscious effort to keep your head fixed rigidly in place.* If you do that you are likely to make a reverse-weight shift, or reverse-pivot.

This ugly fault is rife. Look around at your club. The player who tries to keep his head still fails to rotate his spine correctly, and his weight fills his left shoe as he completes his backswing. Now he is stuck. The only way to get back to the ball is shift his weight to the right side at the start of the downswing. It's a tilt, not a turn. Everything is back to front, and the clubhead is destined to travel along a severely steep outside-to-in path.

Classic symptoms of this fault include pulled and sliced shots, and a general lack of power. If any of this sounds familiar, take a leaf out of my book, and *let your head rotate in tandem with your spine.* You'll feel a whole lot better for it, and your ball-striking will improve in leaps and bounds.

TURNING ON THE POWER – *my key thoughts*

Before we look at a driver sequence in detail and pull out the main power points, let me deal with a couple of questions I often get asked by my pro-am partners. The first is how high should you tee the ball.

Much depends on circumstance. For a regular drive I would tee the ball so that approximately half of it is visible above the top edge of the clubface. That's about right for a powerful upward sweep through impact. Downwind I might tee the ball a little higher in search of a higher flight; into the wind fractionally lower, but don't go too low, or you hit down with too much sidespin. I might also vary the ball position relative to my left instep by an inch or two, depending on the shape I'm looking for. These are the only variables you have to worry about when you set up with a driver, and you should experiment with them to discover what effect the various combinations have on the outcome.

You may have noticed the way I hover the clubhead behind the ball at address. This is a habit I have picked up over the years, but I don't recommend it to everyone. Like many players on tour, I find it helps me to make a wide and smooth takeaway – a prerequisite for a powerful backswing coil. Hovering the clubhead suits me, but it may not suit you.

The second popular question is what difference on the tee is there between a driver swing and a regular iron swing. To that, my answer is nothing in the swing itself, *but the angle of attack is different*. With the iron clubs you are looking for the slightly downward blow that takes ball then divot. With a driver you want to sweep the ball off the peg, and minor adjustments in the set-up position must reflect that intention. Then it's business as usual. When I practise I try not to hit too many drives in succession. I keep a wedge handy and hit a few pitch shots in between. That helps me to maintain my feel and rhythm, and keeps my timing sharp. If there's a sure way of losing your tempo it's firing on all cylinders too hard for too long. You need a cooling off period every now and again. Here are some thoughts to ponder.

THE SET-UP
A solid base for a solid swing

THE TAKEAWAY
Think '*low and slow*' for width

TO THE TOP
Loading the spring

I feel comfortable with a stance that sees the insides of my heels approximately shoulder-width apart. With my knees flexed, I settle my weight 45:55 in favour of the right side, and that sets my right shoulder slightly lower than my left – another sign that my body is geared up to make a powerful turn. I waggle the clubhead a couple of times to stay loose, or 'syrupy' as I call it. I want my muscles to work like strong strands of elastic. You won't hit the ball a long way if you're tense and tight.
Everything must be ready to *flow*.

When I'm hitting it well off the tee my thoughts are focused on getting my upper body behind the ball in the backswing with a good wind-up, and the takeaway holds the key. The trigger I use is *low and slow*. I concentrate on turning my shoulders, my arms and the club away from the ball in one piece, which promotes a wide arc. At the same time I sense that my weight begins to flow across to the right side, and so the coiling process in underway.

Turning your upper body against a flexed right knee is the key to a powerfully coiled backswing position. The spring is now fully loaded – you can almost feel the energy bursting out. I don't like to see the clubshaft get too far past the horizontal at the top. If you check your position side on, you should see a slight cupping in the back of your left hand, and your left thumb should be under the shaft. That's a sign of strength.

THE POWER MOVE
Unwind in sync

In all my years studying the swing, the one solid conclusion to draw is that every great player starts his downswing with a subtle reflexive action in his lower body – usually the left foot or left knee. *My own feeling is that my left knee and left shoulder move together*, and that signals the move towards the target. In that split-second my body is actually moving in two directions at once. My wrists, you will notice, have remained fully hinged throughout.

IMPACT
Rotate left and *collect* the ball

I get a great sense of freedom as I rotate my body through the shot. My body is the engine generating the power, while my arms and hands transmit that energy down through the clubshaft to the ball.

At the very last second, my right shoulder, right hip and right knee fire and add thrust through impact – where speed matters the most. When I practise I often say to myself *left side clears, right side drives*. On a good day I feel that I punish the back of the ball with my right shoulder – that's my power source.

THE FINISH
Wind it all up in balance

Having rotated my body hard through the ball, my chest now faces the target and my spine is vertical. The majority of my weight is now on my left side, and my right foot is balanced up on its toe.

When you commit yourself to a freewheeling release of the clubhead, your hands should finish low behind your neck, while your right shoulder ends up being the closest part of your body to the target. Such a position reflects modern thinking and minimizes the stress on your back.

7
PUTTING
THE PERSONAL TOUCH

Putting is all about controlling your mind.
The secret is to work on the basics, build a repeating stroke,
and then learn to trust and 'let it go'.

Look around the practice green at any professional tournament and you will soon appreciate the fact that putting is a very personal affair. No other aspect of the game is so vulnerable to individual interpretation. Take the set-up. Some players stand tall, others crouch so far over the ball they could almost tie their laces. I've seen scores of fine putters who adopt a quite open stance, and yet there are just as many who stand square to the line. Gary Player, for one, hasn't done so badly with a closed set-up position.

In the never-ending search for the perfect stroke, golfers have tried just about every grip configuration imaginable. There are few rules. It matters not whether you place your right hand below your left, or the left below right. You can join your hands together any way you like. Or you can split them far apart.

One of the world's most deliberate and resilient golfers, Bernhard Langer, has made famous a grip in which he clasps the shaft of his putter against his left forearm with his right hand. It gets the job done. Bernhard is one of the finest touch putters you will ever see.

THE SET-UP – *my keys to consistency*

Now that I have opened the door on the need to experiment until you find a method that is both comfortable and effective, let me say there are a number of factors common to a repeating stroke. Regard these as the parameters of a good putting technique.

First, your posture. It doesn't matter if you are open or closed, but most good putting strokes revolve around a consistent spine angle. You don't see too many top players who lean forward or who have their weight excessively back on their heels. Most of us adopt a vertical spine position.

The pendulum-style method that I use and recommend is controlled predominantly by the bigger muscles in the shoulders, and by its very nature demands a

fairly orthodox set-up position. To give my arms and shoulders the freedom they need to work and interact correctly, I flex my knees, stick my rear end out and bend from the hips until my arms hang naturally in front of my body. Free of tension, the two elbows list in towards my side, and when I bring the palms of my hands together on the grip, the putter becomes merely an extension of my arms.

Check your own position in a mirror, and pay special attention to the way your elbows relate to your body. Comfort has to be a major consideration, but try to make sure that at least one – ideally both – of your elbows rest close in to your side. Most of the good players that I talk to say they like to feel their elbows work back and forth along a 'rail'. That's a useful image to keep in mind.

GOVERNED BY THE SHOULDERS, MY ELBOWS WORK BACK AND FORTH ON A 'RAIL', AND THE STROKE REPEATS ITSELF.

THE GRIP –
two hands joined as one

THE STANDARD
REVERSE-OVERLAP
GRIP IS THE MOST
POPULAR ON TOUR,
BUT YOU SHOULD
EXPERIMENT WITH
THIS AND A RANGE OF
ALTERNATIVES UNTIL
YOU FIND A GRIP THAT
IS BOTH
COMFORTABLE AND
FUNCTIONAL.

Now the grip. Regardless of the way in which you choose to marry your hands together, I believe it's important that you place your palms pretty much parallel to each other and square to the alignment of the putter-face. That way you keep everything *neutral,* and so increase your chances of the putter-face working square to your hands and arms. Jack Nicklaus always sets a weak left hand against a strong right hand. His palms never get to face each other, and yet Nicklaus is one of the greatest pressure putters the game has seen.

With a conventional grip, I tend to regard the left as the guiding hand, while the right is very much responsible for *feeling* the pace of the putt. This is reflected in the way I hold the club as illustrated on the page opposite. The grip runs diagonally through the palm of my left hand, and is secured in position with pressure felt mainly in the last three fingers. That's a firm, not a tight hold. I sense that my left hand has control of the putter, but the muscles in my wrist and forearm are relaxed.

The right hand caresses the club more in the fingers. Again, the trigger unit that is formed between the right thumb and forefinger makes for a sensitive component, and that's something you must foster. To enrich your sense of feel, make sure the pads of each thumb rest lightly on top of the shaft. Treat those as your sensor pads.

As far as the details go, it's up to you to find a method of joining the fingers that is both comfortable and allows you to maintain a consistent pressure in the forearms. That's important. I putt best when the muscles in my forearms are relaxed, so that my hands and arms are able to feel the weight and momentum of the putter-head as I swing it to and fro. Not everyone agrees. Tom Watson has always says that he squeezes the blood out of his grip, so that under pressure he cannot possibly grip it any tighter. And no one holes out better than Tom did in his prime.

Probably the most popular means of joining the hands together is the standard reverse-overlap grip, so called because of the way the left forefinger is draped across the fingers of the right hand. Not only does this feel snug, but that extra support enables the two hands to work as one secure guiding unit. Which is exactly the balance you must strive to achieve.

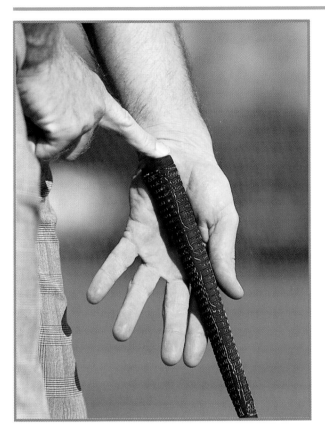

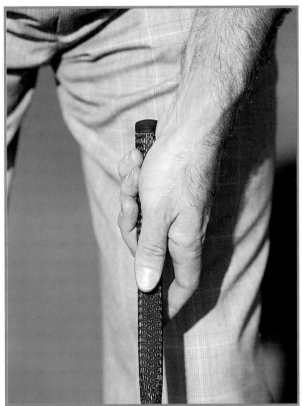

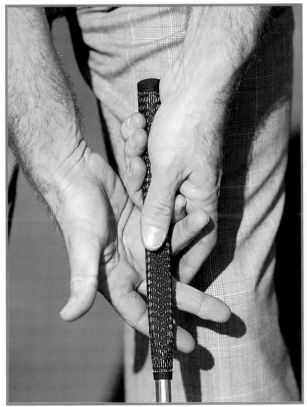

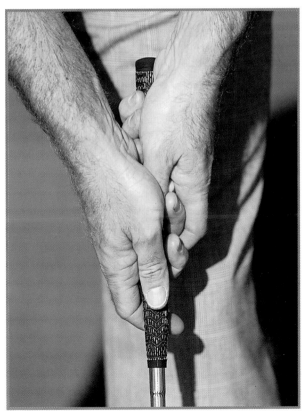

Experiment with the left below right

Of the many options, I suggest that you experiment with the common Vardon grip, and also with the reverse-handed (or 'cack-handed') grip, a relatively new fashion. Placing your left hand below the right certainly has its benefits, and towards the end of the 1994 season, dispirited with my performance on the greens, I decided to give it serious thought. A change is often as good as a rest.

Practising at home, I found the reverse-handed method satisfied a number of the elements I look for in a sound putting stroke. For one thing, the relative position of the hands makes it much easier to get the shoulders level at address, and so promotes a true pendulum-type action. At the same time, placing the left hand below the right automatically positions your right elbow comfortably towards the side of your body, where it remains throughout the stroke.

The truly great putters have always had this connection between their arms and body; the arms don't wander about independently, and the stroke repeats itself. So placed on the shaft, my hands feel soft, and therefore there is less muscular tension running through my arms to the shoulders. I can feel the 'lag' in my hands as I change direction, and as a result I am more positive in swinging and accelerating the putter-head through the ball.

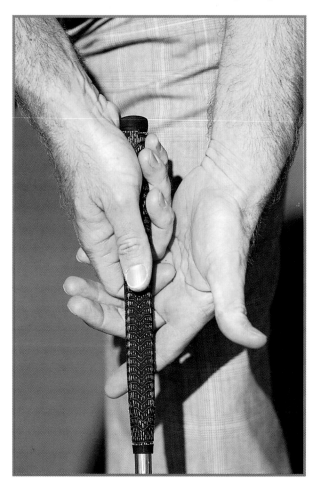
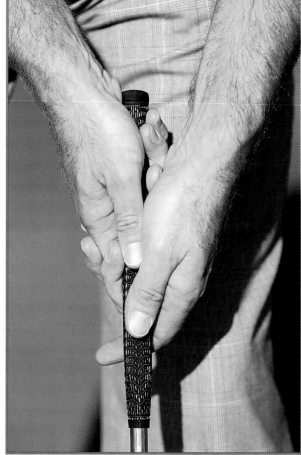

BALL POSITION –
promote upward brushing motion

Rather like planting top-spin on the cue-ball in snooker, the ideal strike in putting is a slightly upward brushing motion, one that catches the ball on or just above the equator, and so sets it rolling *end-over-end*. The ball position relative to your feet has a lot to do with your ability to achieve this. It's certainly no coincidence that most good putters play the ball forward, between the middle of their stance and the inside of the left heel.

I regard this as another of the few rules to observe on the green, and you should check this feature of your set-up on a regular basis. All you need to do is adopt your normal posture, then drop a ball from your left eye and mark where it lands. Play from within an inch or so of that point and you will find that you are able to strike 'up' on the ball freely through impact.

There is another element of the putting technique which I feel can be improved with the help of the reverse-handed grip. As I adopt a stance, look at the way in which my hands and arms fall nicely in towards my body, forming more of a true pendulum with the shoulders. The ball is positioned directly below my eye-line, and as I rock my shoulders to create motion the putter-head travels low to the ground. With a sensation of pulling the putter-head through the ball with the back of my left hand, the face is square all the way through impact. Mechanically, my stroke is *on line for longer*.

Throughout this chapter I shall demonstrate various drills and exercises using both the conventional and cack-handed grips. I believe in both. What you must do is find the method that suits you, and *works*.

THE STROKE – *building a repeatable method*

When I work on the mechanics of my stroke, I often think in terms of the role each part of my body plays. It's a chain reaction. The shoulders control the motion – they create momentum as they rock up and down. My elbows work back and forth along a groove, while my forearms and hands translate this movement into *feel*.

Some people say the hands and wrists should be eliminated from the equation. I don't agree. If you isolate the hands you end up with a 'wooden' stroke and little or no feel. To create the momentum that gets the ball rolling, your hands and wrists must be 'alive' and free to flex and respond naturally. All the best putters have what I call *lag* in their stroke. You watch the players who are winning tournaments and see the speed at which the ball hits the hole. They are *aggressive* through impact, and it is because they nurture that freedom in the wrists and forearms that they are able to achieve this controlled acceleration with a relatively small stroke.

To appreciate this sensation, go away and hit putts right-handed. The weight of the putter-head will act upon your wrist and you won't be able to resist that subtle flexing as you change direction. Sense that you control the movement of the putter with your shoulders, but *feel* the putter-head with your right hand and forearm.

DRILL

Use your shoulders to create momentum

Here's a drill that will help you to develop that sense of feel within the safety of a shoulder-controlled pendulum-type stroke. Adopt your putting stance – use whichever grip feels most comfortable – then trap an umbrella just above your elbows and get a feel for that triangular relationship formed between your hands, arms and shoulders. Keeping the umbrella in place, work on rocking your right shoulder up and down to move the putter-head back and through. Let the mechanism work as a unit. Provided that you keep your head still and your movement oiled with a good rhythm, you should be aware of the connection between your arms, shoulders and body. Set aside just a few minutes each week to work on this drill and pretty soon your stroke will run like clockwork.

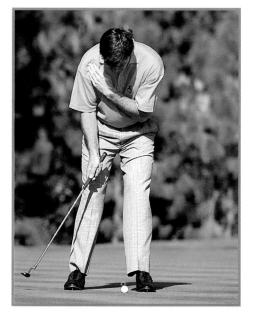

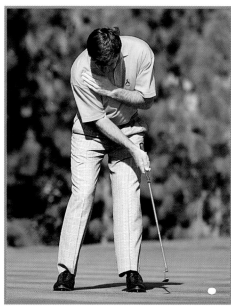

HIT PUTTS WITH YOUR RIGHT HAND ONLY TO APPRECIATE THE SENSATION OF 'LAG' AND ACCELERATION IN YOUR STROKE. THEN RECREATE THAT FEEL WITH YOUR REGULAR GRIP.

HOLING OUT – *keep your putter on the rail*

Let's take it a stage further. On the practice green, find a straight 6-foot putt and work on fine-tuning the mechanics of your pendulum method: rock your shoulders and let your arms and hands respond. Try to keep your head still until you hear the ball rattle in the back of the hole, and hold your follow-through position. Then check that the putter-face has remained square to the path of your stroke. There should be no twisting or turning. A useful tip is to concentrate on keeping your right elbow close to your body. That prevents the putter from wavering about, and so helps you to groove a consistent path. Again, I'm sure this is one of the reasons why so many players are turning to the reverse-handed grip from short range. Placing the right hand above the left automatically positions the right elbow close to your body. Through the stroke, your arms work back and forth on that 'rail'.

Long has been the debate on whether the putter should work on a straight line back and through or follow a gentle curve. For me, the issue is crystal clear. Unless you choose to manipulate the course of the putter with wrist action, the putter-head will trace a natural curve inside the ball-to-target line as it swings back and forth. Simple laws of physics explain that.

RELEASE AND HOLD – KEEP YOUR HEAD STILL UNTIL THE BALL HITS THE BACK OF THE HOLE.

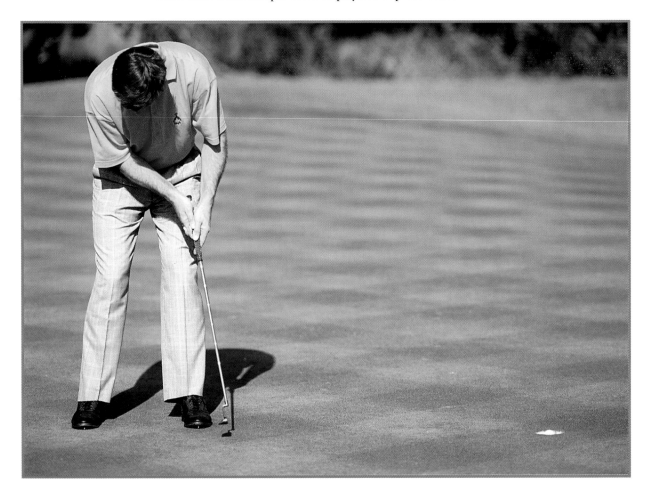

However, I believe that on short putts, up to around 6 or 8 feet on a good surface, it is quite legitimate to work on keeping the putter-head pretty much square to the path going back and through. It will move only fractionally to the inside of the ball-to-target line.

To monitor the path of the putter-head as I swing it back and forth towards the hole, I sometimes mark out a chalk line on the practice green and work on holing 4- and 5-footers. I concentrate on keeping the putter-head low to the ground on the backswing, then on gliding it squarely through impact and up towards the hole. The pace of the stroke is critical. More short putts are missed through a lack of tempo than anything else, so as you work on holing out, try to feel that your hands and the putter-head move at the same speed.

Another useful exercise is to run the putter-head back and forth on top of a shaft. I do this in hotel rooms all around the world, and indeed there are no rules to stop you doing it out on the course whenever you feel your stroke needs a quick examination. When you make a good stroke, the putter is seen to move fractionally inside the shaft as you swing it back, but through to the target you should work on 'chasing' the line. Think *right shoulder up, right shoulder under*. If you set up to the shaft correctly, with your eyes and shoulders square, it's actually quite difficult to get too far off track.

In the run-up to the Open Championship at Muirfield in 1992 I worked particularly hard on holing out from close range. I was determined to keep the putter-head travelling squarely along the line to the hole, and one of the drills I hit upon proved particularly useful. It works like this. Find a straight 3-foot putt and rehearse brushing the ball into the back of the cup, but *without the benefit of a backswing*. Get the feeling of the right hand and forearm pushing the putter-head towards the hole, and check that it's square.

In tandem with these practice techniques, try stroking a few short putts with the leading edge of your wedge or sand iron. Choke down on the grip, and aim to strike the ball just above the equator, so that you get the ball rolling *end-over-end*. The beauty of this exercise is that you are forced to make a low, smooth, backswing and a positive ascending stroke through impact. Which is exactly what you should be looking to achieve with your putter. A good rhythm is mandatory.

  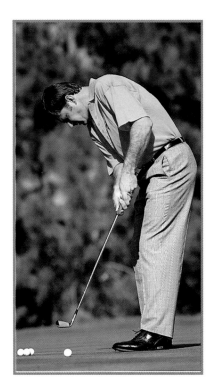

Now let's put all this hard work to the test. Find a hole that is cut on a slight incline and circle four balls around it at the points of a compass. Start with short ones, two or three feet. Take a look at each putt, just as you would on the course, and then hole as many as you can in succession. Set yourself a target and try to beat it. Challenge your nerve. When I do this I concentrate mostly on keeping my head still and rap the ball firmly into the back of the hole. I don't believe in babying putts. If you dribble the ball, then the slightest imperfection or spike mark on the green is liable to throw it off course. Far better to focus your eyes on the back of the ball and commit yourself to making a positive stroke.

One of the most common and destructive faults in putting is that of the left wrist collapsing through impact, and again this is a problem I believe the reverse-handed grip can help to eliminate. With the left hand below the right I am aware of a rock-solid position of the left hand and wrist throughout the stroke - the left wrist guides and mirrors the putter-face as I pull it through the ball, and I try to keep my head still at least until the ball is out of my peripheral vision. It all boils down to trust, but if you practise often enough you will learn to do it out on the course. I might have overdone the 'head still' bit over the years, but I don't often miss from inside six feet.

THE ACID TEST – STROKING PUTTS WITH THE LEADING EDGE OF YOUR WEDGE REINFORCES THE IMPORTANCE OF RHYTHM AS YOU ACCELERATE 'UP' AND THROUGH THE BALL.

LAG PUTTING – *lengthen your stroke and roll the ball*

One thing good putters have in common is the ability to judge distance and roll the ball a dead weight to the hole. They have genuine *feel*. This is not something you achieve overnight, but you can accelerate the learning process with one or two well-chosen drills. The golden rule to remember when you work on the longer putts is that the speed at which you release and roll the ball must be determined by the length of your stroke. The principles governing the way you make that stroke remain unchanged. Whether I face a 6-footer or a tram-liner across the green, I work on the principles of pendulum motion: as the length of the putt increases, so does the length of my swing.

For me, tempo is the key factor. Just as I believe in maintaining an even tempo with every club in the bag, my putting stroke is made with the same unhurried rhythm, no matter how far I have to roll the ball. I make it a habit to swing the putter-head back and forth at a smooth, even pace, relaxing my arms and wrists to such an extent that the putter is encouraged to accelerate smoothly.

When I practise I often say to myself 'one-two' in time with my stroke: 'one' as I take the putter away, 'two' as I swing it along the target line through impact. On another day I might say 'shoulders-shoulders', or 'square-square' on the shorter putts. It makes no difference what you work on, just make sure that you develop a tempo that repeats itself. Believe me, you will hole more putts with a bad stroke and a good tempo than you will with a perfect stroke and no tempo.

Advice David Leadbetter gave me will also help you to release the putter freely on putts of any significant distance. He suggests standing taller, which certainly promotes a flowing pendulum action. The key is to give yourself plenty of room to swing the putter back and forth with a long sweeping stroke that gets the ball rolling with that hint of topspin.

Probably the best way to develop your feel for distance is to go out and stick tee-pegs in the green at 10, 20 and 30 feet, then work between them at random. Vary the length of your stroke to suit the length of the putt, and concentrate on striking the ball out of the middle of the putter-face. You get only one chance on the course, so get it right first time in practice. I sometimes take this drill a stage further, and hit a few balls with my eyes closed. You can do this at home. When you lose one of your senses the others sharpen up to compensate, and so very quickly your overall sense of feel is put on the alert.

Another favourite drill is to lay out a line of balls over a distance of 20 or 40 feet. I place them at intervals of 2 or 3 feet, and then, starting with the shortest putt, work my way back from the hole. The interesting thing about this exercise is that there comes a time when you move from being *technique* conscious to *feel* conscious. At first, say up to a distance of about 20 feet, all I am thinking about is holing the putt. But gradually my goals change. From about 25 or 30 feet I begin to think more in terms of laying the ball close for a safe 2-putt. I watch the way each putt reacts as it rolls across the green, and subsequent putts are made with the benefit of that feedback.

Gradually moving away from the hole 'ladder-fashion' is especially useful as part of a warm-up session before a game. It makes you concentrate. Pretty soon you get a feel for the pace of the greens and a good idea of the subtle breaks and borrows that might exist. Valuable information that you need to putt with a degree of confidence out on the course.

WORK ON THE PRINCIPLES OF PENDULUM MOTION: AS THE LENGTH OF THE PUTT INCREASES, SO MUST THE LENGTH OF YOUR STROKE. ALWAYS VISUALIZE THE BALL RUNNING TWO FEET PAST THE HOLE, AND REMEMBER, AS THE BALL DIES, SO IT WILL TAKE MORE BREAK.

VISUALIZATION – *the art of reading greens*

WHEN YOU FACE A
CURLING PUTT,
VISUALIZE THE LINE
TO THE HOLE AND
FOCUS ON THE POINT
AT WHICH YOU
BELIEVE THE BALL
WILL FIRST TAKE THE
BREAK. IF YOU MAKE
THAT YOUR TARGET,
ALL YOU HAVE TO
WORRY ABOUT IS PACE.

Only through experience will you learn the art of reading the contours on a green correctly. That's not something I can teach you through the pages of a book. What I can do is give you a piece of advice that helped me tremendously as a youngster, and it is simply this: no matter how many subtle breaks and borrows there are to navigate, treat every putt as a straight putt. I am particularly keen to stress this point because so many amateur players seem to struggle with the long- and medium-range approach putts. Trust me, you simplify the problem immediately when you visualize the line to the hole and focus on the point at which the ball will first begin to break. That's your intermediate target – the apex of the putt.

I hardly need add that pace is the governing factor when it comes to reading a line. The harder you strike the ball the less it will take the borrow; hit the ball too softly and it falls miserably away from the line. For me, the ideal pace is that which would send the ball about 18 inches to 2 feet past the hole. That gives the ball a good chance of holding its line. And if I do miss the putt, I will at least have a good idea of the amount of break to play on the return. Leave your putts short of the hole and you are none the wiser.

A point that is often overlooked is the fact that on a curling putt, the centre of the hole actually changes. Think about it. If you study the line of a hard-breaking left-to-right putt, in your mind's eye you would see the ball enter the hole from the left edge as you look at it. If the middle of the hole is normally represented by 6 o'clock, that severe left-to-right slope could make the effective centre nearer to 9 o'clock. It's important that you bear this in mind.

One more thing. I guarantee you will improve your putting the very next time you play if you concentrate on rolling every putt on the high side of the hole. So, if there is left-to-right break, err to the left and be positive with your stroke. Release the putter-head, and hold your position solid. Such a disciplined follow-through actually enhances the quality of your strike. The ball has a chance of dropping in if it dies above the hole, no chance at all if it runs out of steam on the low side.

STRATEGY – *just a routine job to do*

The 5-footer I left myself on the eighteenth green at Muirfield in 1987 was the most pressure-laden putt I have ever had to face. In the process of grinding out 17 pars, I had holed several putts of a similar distance. Then, to win my first major championship, I had to face 'one of those'.

I made that putt because I treated it like any other. I lined it up the same way I lined up any other short putt that day and made my customary practice strokes to the side of the ball. I swamped my mind with thoughts of tempo, and told myself to keep my head still. The cardinal error is to change the way you play just because you happen to find yourself facing a critical shot or putt. As soon as you do that you build tension. So don't go looking for a break from all angles if normally a quick look from either side of the hole does the job. Don't make a dozen practice strokes if normally you are happy with just one or two. And don't freeze over the ball – see the putt and hit it. Develop a routine, and *stick to that routine*.

Once you have the line of the putt in your mind it's all about tempo and keeping your head still. If you lose your tempo and start peeking, you've had it. Stand there and follow your learned procedure to the letter. Swing the putter the way you've swung it a thousand times on the practice green and think positive. The worst that can happen is to miss. I read somewhere that at a university

in America it has been proved that a machine can be set up to hit a 10-foot putt, and only make 7 out of 10. So don't be too hard on yourself.

Concentration plays a huge part. The great Jack Nicklaus is an example to us all in that respect. Look at film of Nicklaus in his prime tournament years. When he gets down to a putt, it's as if he enters his own little world. He immerses himself in a cocoon of concentration, and nothing can break the spell. A phenomenal skill. Such application is often what separates the good from the great putters, perhaps a single-figure player from the middle-order club golfer.

Ultimately, the key is to focus on the putt to the exclusion of all else around you. In your mind's eye, you must learn to see the ball going in the hole even before you've hit it. Even if you should miss, you ought to be able to walk off every green satisfied that you did all you could to make the putt. In the past I may have tried to do too much. I have sometimes suffered a tendency to fiddle about on the greens. Not any more. Whether I am using the reverse-handed method or putting conventionally, my strategy is simple: I line up, aim the putter, take two looks at the hole and bang, it's gone. I trust my stroke and let it go.

I'VE HIT PLENTY OF 'PERFECT' PUTTS THAT HAVE MISSED THE HOLE. THAT'S GOLF. AT LEAST I KNOW THAT EVERY TIME I STRIKE THE BALL I'VE FULFILLED MY HALF OF THE BARGAIN.

8

CHIPPING AND PITCHING

MY SHORT GAME SYSTEM

*No matter how well you strike the ball,
it is your ability to turn three shots into two that ultimately
makes or breaks your score.*

At the end of each tournament week I sit down and analyze my playing statistics from the detailed record I keep of the number of fairways and greens hit in regulation, sand saves, chipping and putting averages, and so on. It's useful homework.

By and large, the full-swing stats vary the least. I'm not the longest on tour, but my driving accuracy is usually pretty good, and on average I hit around 13 out of 18 greens in regulation. My ball-striking in that regard is fairly consistent. So why do I shoot 68 one day, 72 the next?

The figures say it all. Week in and week out it is the quality of my short game, all the shots played within wedge range – which for me is up to 125 yards from the flag – that determines how well I score. If I'm sharp, I expect to get up-and-down when I miss a green, and pounce on good birdie opportunities with a pitch and a putt. But as soon as I lose my touch, shots slip away. What should have been a par becomes a bogey, birdies are missed, and so the mood changes. Recognize a similar pattern in your own game?

Gathering such information would be of little use if I didn't act upon it, and certainly I spend more time around the practice green than I do beating balls on the range. I experiment with the basic short game techniques to define a host of scoring shots – running the ball one minute, throwing it high the next. There is such scope for imagination, and no substitute for regular practice.

In this game, a lack of vision and creativity is often what separates a good from a great player. So as you go to work on the following skills, I want you always to be inventive. Vary your position around the flag, *see* the shot you intend to play, then pull it off.

THE 'CHIP-PUTT' – *as simple as it is effective*

The short game system I have developed is based on a simple philosophy: *wherever possible, keep the ball close to the ground*. It would be very easy for me to reach for my sand iron and throw the ball high at the flag every time I missed a green, but why take such a risk? It's much easier – and *safer* – to judge distance with a simple bump-and-run. Based on my normal putting action, this rather cheeky chip-putt technique often fits the bill when I find my ball just a few feet off the edge of the green. Using a mid- to short-iron I can loft the ball over any broken ground, and thus eliminate possible uncertainty. I aim to land the ball about a yard beyond the fringe, and then read the line to the hole just like a long putt.

The way I set up to the shot clearly reflects my intentions. Choking down on the shaft for control, I use my regular putting grip and adopt a comfortably narrow and slightly open stance. I huddle my body like I would to make a long putt – that enhances my feel – and with my eyes directly over the ball I make sure that my shoulders are square to the target line. Leaning gently towards the target, my weight might just favour the left side.

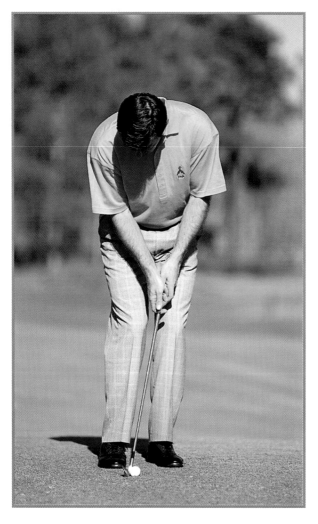

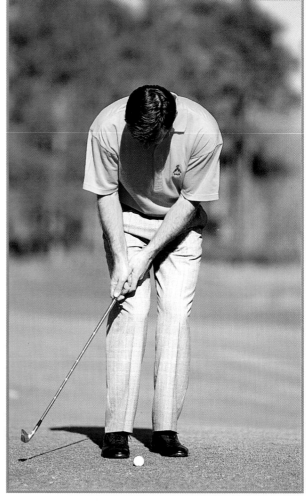

Notice the way the club sits up on its toe at address. That's deliberate. Striking the ball towards the toe-end of the clubface helps to 'deaden' impact, which makes it easier for you to judge the speed at which the ball releases and runs on the green.

From this position I can make a simple, uninhibited pendulum-like stroke with my arms and shoulders. A light grip pressure gives me a little flex in my wrists as I change direction, but essentially the wrists remain passive throughout. Standing slightly open helps me to release the clubhead freely towards the hole, and the ball is neatly pinched off the turf. Under strict control, it pops forward, hops once and then checks before rolling out towards the hole.

I suggest that you sharpen your touch with just three clubs – start with a 6-iron, 8-iron and wedge – and switch between these at random to develop a versatile system. The key is to focus on landing each ball a similar distance on the green, and work on repeating a fluent stroke. With the relatively straight-faced 6-iron, the ball will come out low and run maybe 30 or 40 feet, depending on the quality of the surface. The 8-iron flies a little higher, and rolls slightly less, while the same easy stroke with a wedge produces a softer pop-up shot that stops quickly, the perfect solution when the hole is cut within 10 or 15 feet of the fringe.

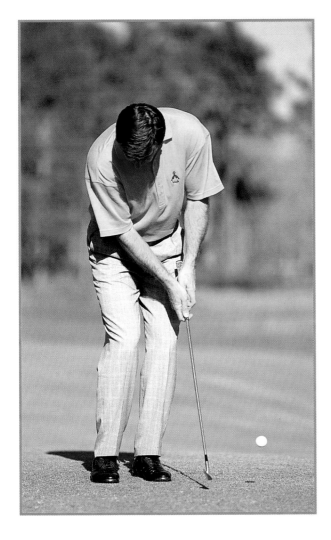

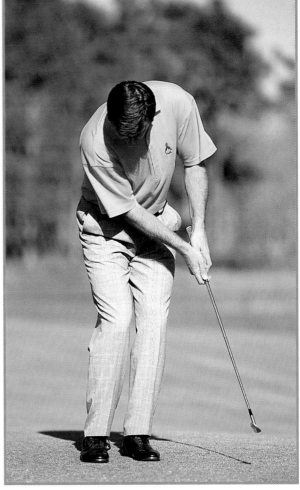

THE CHIPPING STROKE – *a versatile technique*

I like the way the chip-putt teaches you the simplicity of the chipping principle. But it is limited to shots around the very edge of the green. As you move further out, the length of your swing and the amount of wrist action you employ must reflect the distance you have to fly the ball. The key is knowing how to adjust your set-up position so that you are able to blend good technique with *feel*, and really there are just two small changes to make.

First, you need to stand taller at address, so that your arms are free to hang in front of your body. Second, you switch to your normal grip.

For a regular chip shot I would again choke down on the club – in this example I'm playing a 9-iron – and set my body quite open to the target line. That gives my arms the room they need to swing freely and release the club towards the hole. Playing the ball back in the rear part of my stance automatically places my hands forward, and to consolidate that position I flex my knees and lean ever so gently towards the target.

Having effectively preset impact, the key to making a good swing is to focus entirely on the top of your body. Your shoulders, arms and hands – in that order – do all the work. It's a chain reaction.

To set the wheels in motion, turn your shoulders and let your arms and hands flow back and forth in response to their momentum. As long as you maintain a sensitive grip pressure you should feel your wrists hinge gently to add a silky smooth *lag* between backswing and downswing. That's the secret to

a classical chipping action. Whether your swing is long or short, cultivating that 'play' in your wrists enables you to control the speed of the clubhead through impact. Let your arms and hands lead the way and feel the clubhead nip the ball and gently bruise the turf.

Some people say the wrists should be passive in chipping, but I don't agree. If you isolate the wrists, your stroke will feel wooden. You want your swing to have *flow*, and that quality stems from the natural hinging and flexing of your wrist muscles as you change direction.

Take a bag of balls and work on developing this subtle art. Concentrate on making the same smooth stroke each time, and switch between clubs to vary the trajectory of your shots. Think in terms of controlling the length and speed of your swing with the rotary motion of your trunk – that's a useful image. Let your wrists hinge naturally to complement your overall rhythm, and hold on to your finish as you watch the shot unfold.

EXPERIMENT WITH A SPAN OF CLUBS AND DEVELOP YOUR AWARENESS IN THIS CRITICAL SCORING RANGE.

CONTROL DISTANCE WITH TRAJECTORY

A SENSE OF CONTROL –
'ROLL' YOUR RIGHT
HAND FOR A LOW
RUNNER . . .

I could fill a whole chapter with the variations that are possible in chipping, but that would spoil your fun. Now you have the basis of a good stroke, go out and discover the different ways you can use it to feed the ball towards the hole. Challenge not just your technique, but your imagination.

Start off just a few yards from the edge of the green, and work the span between your 6-iron and your wedge to get a feel for the ratio of flight-to-roll that each club gives you. Vary the distance to your target, and hit four or five shots with each club. For the majority of shots around the green I tend to use a 6-iron, 8-iron or wedge. I practise with these clubs so often that I understand exactly what sort of shot each one gives me, and then I apply that knowledge out on the course.

To guarantee a predictable first bounce, I usually aim to land the ball a couple of yards on to the green, and then picture the line to the hole from there. With a lot of green to work with – say 30 or 40 feet – I would choose to play the straight-faced clubs – a 6- or 8-iron – and visualize a shot that spends considerably more time on the ground than it does in the air. If the hole were cut tight to the edge of the green, my strategy would be different. I would take a

lofted wedge and play a shot that carries the fringe and then sits down quickly. But the basic chipping technique would remain the same. Go out and establish your own sliding scale.

As your confidence grows you can be more ambitious. Try to *work* the ball. Imagine you are playing a mini-draw, and feel your right hand roll over your left through impact. That encourages the ball to run with overspin, which can be useful when you have to play a shot into the wind, or run the ball up a slope.

At the other end of the scale you may need the ball to check up a little more than normal, so work on a slicing action that produces backspin. To do that you should play the ball forward in your stance and make a conscious effort to hold the clubface open through impact. This time you want your right hand to work *beneath* the left; there is no crossing over. In fact, a good feeling to have is that you pull the heel of the club across the ball, keeping your left wrist firm.

Trial and error is the only way to better your education as a golfer. Feel and remember the different sensations associated with hitting the ball high, low and all stops in between. Vary the length and pace of your swing to play shots that either run quickly or walk slowly. These skills add a whole new dimension to your short game.

... HOLD THE CLUBFACE OPEN TO PLAY A HIGHER, FLOATING SHOT.

Pitch shots – *think 'stomach and buttons'*

The short game really is a family affair. From the putting stroke we developed the chip-putt. Out of the chip-putt evolved the regular chipping swing. And now, simply by extending the length of the swing and working on a more pronounced wrist action, we enter the realm of the pitch shot – the way I fly the ball through the air from up to 40 and 80 yards out.

Working with a wedge or sand iron, I again like to stand with my feet and hips open to the target, but the further I move away from the green, the more I set my shoulders square to the line. That helps me to swing the club back and forth on a good plane. For a regular shot I play the ball in the middle of my feet, and as I flex my knees my weight again favours the left side. Rehearse this position in front of a mirror.

Above all, it's important that you relax over the ball. Grip an inch or so down the shaft for added control, and let your arms hang comfortably in front of your chest – make them feel extra *heavy*.

Now that you are ready to play, the key is to turn your upper body over the support of your knees and hips, and work on setting the club on plane with a good wrist action. You are using one of the most upright clubs in your bag, so your swing will naturally tend to be quite steep. When you set the club correctly in the backswing it should feel quite light and *balanced*. That's a sure sign your swing is on the right track, and from there you can be fairly confident of achieving the positive ball-turf strike which characterizes a good pitch shot.

With a premium on accuracy, I think in terms of repeating a three-quarter length swing, and control my acceleration through the ball with the rotary motion of my body. The swing thought I use is 'stomach and buttons'. I focus on turning my stomach away from the ball, then try to finish with my shirt buttons facing the hole. That gets my upper body working correctly, and also helps me to establish a good rhythm. Work on this when you practise. If you can learn to control the length of your swing with the rotary motion of your body, your ability to gauge both the distance and trajectory of your shots will improve dramatically.

CONTROLLING THE LENGTH OF YOUR SWING WITH THE ROTARY MOTION OF YOUR TRUNK, YOU CAN ACCELERATE THROUGH THE BALL WITH THE EMPHASIS ON THE SPEED OF YOUR BODY, AND NOT ON THE SPEED OF YOUR HANDS.

How to improve your ball-striking

Good players are always aggressive from pitching range. My Ryder Cup team-mate José Maria Olazabal is a good example. Watch him, and see how he rips through the ball and peppers the flag with spin. The Zimbabwean Nick Price is another with a neat, clinical technique. The key is that they trust the clubface, and commit themselves to striking *down and through* the ball.

Here's a drill that can help you get aggressive. Set up as I described to play the regular pitch shot, then raise your right heel an inch or so off the ground, and *keep it raised as you work on your swing*. With the majority of your weight now supported on your left side, all you have to think about is turning your upper body back and through towards the target. Remember the cue: 'stomach and buttons'.

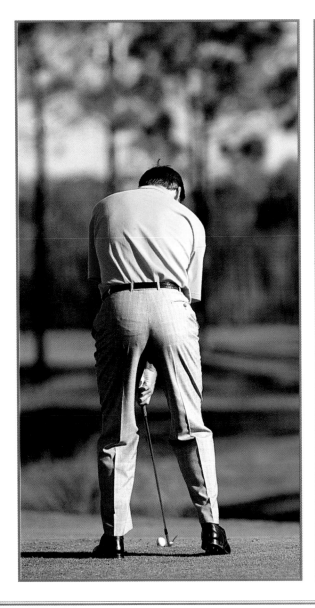

Turn your stomach first away from and then towards the target, and let your arms respond naturally. Hinge your wrists like you always do, and make a conscious effort to strike *down and through* the ball. Don't be afraid of hitting hard. Take a wedge or sand wedge and try to rip out little 3-inch divots (that's a sliver, not a thick steak). Get a feel for the grip you put on the ball. As long as you keep your left forearm travelling at the same speed as your stomach through impact, you can be certain that the clubface will be in the correct position to give you a crisp ball-turf strike. Finish your swing in balance, with your body straight and eyes forward. As the quality of your ball-striking improves you will find that even with a low trajectory you can play pitch shots of between 60 and 100 yards and stop the ball quickly on the green.

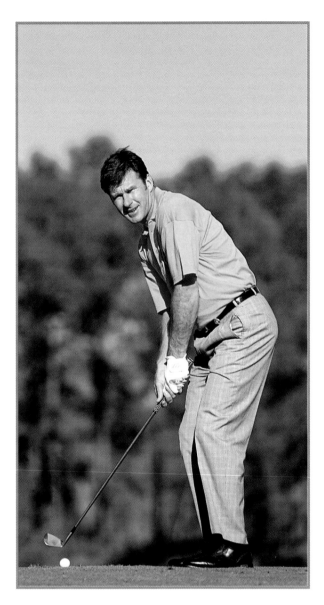

THE PUNCH SHOT – *a lethal weapon*

In the process of developing your short game skills you will find that you keep coming back to a favourite type of shot. Mine is the punch wedge. It's a subtle variation of the basic pitching technique, where the clubface is 'held off' through the ball to produce a low-flying, heavily spinning shot. I use it from that sometimes awkward 50- to 80-yard range, primarily to beat the wind.

Like I do in most of my shots from close range, I set up with my weight slightly favouring my left side, the ball positioned just back of centre in my stance and my hands forward. Again, everything is geared for impact. The key is to return to this position at speed, so that the ball is punched forward.

The movement of my arms is again governed by the engine room of my shoulders and upper body. Restricting myself to a compact, three-quarter length

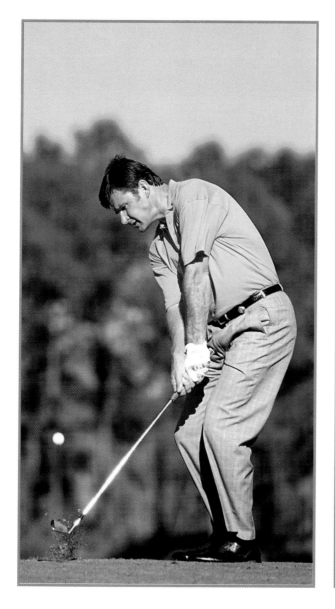

swing, I focus on hinging my wrists early on the way back so the club is set on plane, and then on holding that angle in my wrists all the way through impact. Keeping my weight on the left side promotes the steep downswing attack that I need to 'trap' the ball against the turf. The feeling I have is that my upper body 'covers' the shot, while my hands and forearms dominate the clubhead.

This distinctive punching action is best understood front-on as I complete my swing. See how my body clears and my hands and forearms pull *across left* through the ball; the clubhead is not allowed to pass my hands as I make a restricted three-quarter finish, my chest now facing the target. The ball flies with a low piercing trajectory, skips once, and then settles down quickly on the second bounce.

CONTROLLING THE TRAJECTORY OF YOUR SHOTS IS THE KEY TO PLAYING IN THE WIND. THE DISTINCTIVE PUNCH TECHNIQUE ENABLES YOU TO FLY THE BALL NO MORE THAN 20 FEET IN THE AIR, AND STILL STOP IT QUICKLY ON THE GREEN.

DRILL

Use a towel and stay 'connected'

A recurring theme throughout this book has been the emphasis I place on controlling the length of my swing with the bigger and more dependable muscles in my body. The short game is no exception, and the towel drill is the best exercise I know for tightening up and grooving a good pitching technique. But remember, it is only designed for the short shots – up to 50 or 60 yards at the most.

It works like this. Trap the ends of a towel under the upper part of each arm, then take your regular set-up position and work on making a smooth, three-quarter length swing. Let your wrists hinge naturally to keep the club on plane, and get used to the feeling of *linkage* as you turn the top half of your body over the resistance of your knees and hips. Keep the towel in place as you swing back and through.

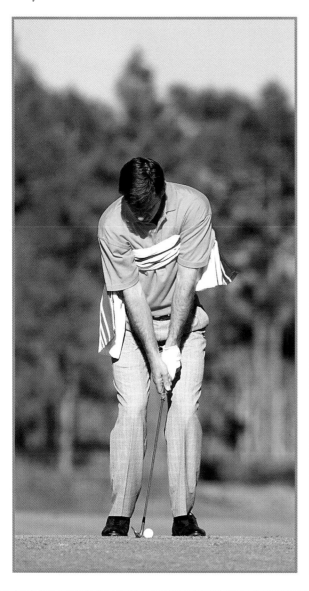

When I do this my thoughts are geared towards making a pure strike and swinging the clubhead to a balanced finish. There is a ball-turf contact, but as long as I rotate my arms and turn my chest correctly, the attack is a fairly shallow one. I don't believe in taking a big divot. That only complicates your ability to judge distance. Remember, swing easy, fly it soft.

David Leadbetter once suggested that I should use my body speed to control both the distance I hit the ball and the amount of spin I put on my pitch shots. He told me to imagine a 40-yard pitch as requiring a 40 mph swing, 50 yards needing 50 mph, and so on. This *speedometer principle* is certainly effective. Focusing on the rotary speed of your body conjures up a graphic mental image that you can use any time you need to play a 'part' shot. The speed at which you release the clubhead also determines the amount of spin you put on the ball: the faster you release the club, the more backspin you generate, and *vice versa*.

THE FULL WEDGE –
how to regulate spin and distance

I usually carry a standard 49-degree pitching wedge, a utility wedge with 53 degrees of loft, and a special 60-degree sand iron. That gives me a fair amount of flexibility to flight shots high at the pin. The key is to find pitching clubs that you like the look of, and then discover your 'best lengths' with each one. For me, a full pitching wedge flies about 125 yards. But my best length, with what I call a 'controlled full hit' would be 120 yards. Similarly, while a full swing with my middle wedge has a range of 110 yards, my best length with that club is 105 yards. That's where I'm most accurate. The 60-degree sand iron has a range of just 75 yards, but again the best length for me is just shy of that, at 70 yards.

My favourite attacking shot is the 105-yard wedge. That's the one I go looking for out on the course. On a short par-4, I figure out how far I have to hit my tee shot to leave myself with 105 yards to the flag. Similarly, if a par-5 is out of range in two shots, I think in terms of laying up to that 105-yard line.

This yardage game is a key element of professional strategy, and it's something you should pick up on. Get yourself two or three wedges you feel comfortable with, and practise until you can accurately gauge how far you hit each club. These shots are critical in terms of your ability to score.

Work on the in-between shots, too. No matter how carefully you plot your way around a course you will find yourself between clubs, and so you need to know how to vary your distances. There are a couple of ways you can do this, the easiest being simply to choke down on the grip. Try going down the shaft progressively by one, two and even three inches. With every step you effectively shorten the length of the shaft, so without having to adjust your swing you automatically restrict your clubhead speed and produce shots that fly less through the air. That's the beauty of this method: once you have made the necessary adjustment, you can still afford to be aggressive through the ball.

I should add that each time I shorten my grip on the club I also narrow my stance and move the ball progressively back in my stance, towards my right foot. All this helps to improve my sense of control.

Here's a more advanced technique. Taking the speedometer principle a stage further, I like to gauge the length of my shots and vary the spin I put on the ball with the speed of my delivery through impact. If I want to hit a shot that spins and stops quickly I work on releasing the clubhead with a brisk, upbeat tempo. By contrast, if I want to play a shot that trundles a few yards on the green, I quieten my body action. That has the effect of reducing my speed through impact, and the result is a softer flight with less spin.

In a nutshell, that ability to control your acceleration through the ball – and to *feel* it – is the key to a good short game. Listen to the sound the ball makes coming off the clubface and learn to associate certain sounds with certain types of shot. Be creative. Don't be afraid to juggle about with the variables of ball position and weight distribution. This is something I do to pass the time on the practice tee, and it teaches you a great deal about spin and control.

If I want to lower the trajectory of my shots, I set up with the ball in the rear part of my stance, and let my weight favour the left side. In the swing itself I then feel my upper body dominates the shot. I focus on making a full shoulder turn and swing the club more *around* my body than normal, both going back and through. That rotation is felt at impact, as the clubhead turns over the ball and sends it flying low with a low draw. I finish the job with a compact, three-quarter length follow through.

To play a higher shot I simply open my stance, settle my weight more evenly between my feet and move the ball forwards. These adjustments automatically place my hands behind the ball and increase the effective loft on the clubface. The swing is now very much a hands and arms affair. I try to keep my body still

and quiet. The open clubface costs you distance, so you need to hit these shots hard. The ball will tend to fly with a touch of left-to-right spin, so be sure that you make the necessary allowances.

If you exaggerate these adjustments to play a high ball you very soon enter the realm of the lob shot, which has to be one of the most satisfying recoveries in golf. You need a good cushion of grass to play this shot, but if conditions are in your favour you can make the ball climb almost vertically and stop very quickly.

With a wedge or sand iron, open up both your stance and the clubface, just as if you were about to play a regular bunker shot, and keep your hands and wrists relaxed. The key is to then focus on setting your wrists fairly early in the backswing, and hold on to that angle as you pull the open clubface through impact. Again, use the rotation of your body to control the speed of the delivery; keep your movements smooth, and aim to cut the legs from beneath the ball. Confidence in playing this shot will quickly boost your confidence out of the sand.

Work on these thoughts on the practice ground and find out just how versatile – and *accurate* – you can be with your short irons. These are the skills you need to combat ever-changing conditions and to shoot for the pin.

WITH A WEDGE IN YOUR HANDS, EXPERIMENT WITH THE VARIABLES OF ALIGNMENT AND BALL POSITION UNTIL YOU FEEL COMFORTABLE PUNCHING A SHOT LOW, OR LOBBING A BALL HIGH.

9

SAND SCHOOL

The skill of a great bunker player is understanding how the ball
will react from a certain lie, and visualizing the shot accordingly.

I am much happier in the bunker than I am playing a recovery shot out of tangly greenside rough. Assuming a good, clean lie, I can afford to be quite aggressive in the sand. I know I can spin the ball, and fully expect it to finish close to the hole. Out of the rough you always live in danger of catching a 'flier' – even on the shortest of shots – and that element of uncertainty does little to enhance your sense of control and confidence.

Control – for me, that's the key word. If there is a secret to a polished short game it is understanding the way the ball reacts from different lies around the green, and then developing your awareness of the clubhead to the extent that you are able to control impact. Sand shots are unique in this respect. Utilizing what's known as the 'bounce effect', the idea here is that you use your sand iron to cut a shallow divot of sand from *beneath* the ball, and thus propel it up into the air. The clubhead doesn't actually touch the ball. Using the sand as a buffer, you do literally splash it out.

If your bunker play costs you rather than saves you, cancel your next game and spend a couple of hours working on the following ideas and drills. That's all the time it will take for you to grasp the fundamental skills. As your confidence grows, your expectations will rise. You won't be happy with just hitting the green, you'll be looking to knock the ball close to the hole. Just like the pro.

THE SPLASH SHOT – *First, open the clubface*

In terms of your ability to put together a good score, the regular splash shot is perhaps *the* most important recovery in golf. The textbook calls for a shallow swing that slides the open clubface beneath the ball. And as simple as this sounds, the way you form your grip holds the key.

Let me show you what I mean. For a regular greenside shot I stand about 30 degrees open to the target, and settle down with my weight slightly favouring my left side. I flex my knees and shuffle my shoes into the sand until my body is firmly anchored. With the ball positioned opposite my left

YOUR SAND IRON IS DESIGNED IN SUCH A WAY THAT THE BACK OF THE FLANGE IS SET LOWER THAN THE LEADING EDGE. THAT FEATURE OF THE CLUB CREATES THE 'BOUNCE EFFECT' – BUT ONLY IF YOU KNOW HOW TO USE IT PROPERLY.

instep, *I then swivel the grip through my fingers until the clubface is open in relation to my body but square with the line to the flag.* Then I complete my grip and settle down to play the shot. I cannot stress too strongly the importance of this procedure: open the clubface first, *then* form your grip. To get into the habit of doing this properly it might not be a bad idea if you take the club first in your right hand, and simply twiddle the shaft through your fingers until the clubface is open. Then apply your left hand and make your grip. Compare your set-up to mine.

Follow your body, and keep that face open

Having effectively preset a good impact position, making the swing is easy. You simply follow the line of your body. Focus your eyes on a spot a couple of inches behind the ball – that's your point of entry – and slice out a cushion of sand. Keep your arms and wrists relaxed as you turn your shoulders back and through, and hold your finish to inspire rhythm and balance.

Don't worry too much about aiming at a target when you first go out to practise these shots. Hit a few balls and get used to the sensation of opening and swinging the clubface across the line. Be aggressive.

To regulate distance I work on the theory that you should aim to take a consistent cut of sand, but vary the speed at which you release the clubhead through impact. You will recognize this as the same 'speedometer principle' I use to gauge my pitching distance off the fairway. Within this system I also tinker with the angle of the clubface to suit a particular shot. For example, if the hole was cut tight to the bunker, I would probably lay the face wide open. If I needed the ball to run I would be inclined to square it up a fraction.

You have all this fun to discover. Go out and mix these ingredients together to establish your personal range. Just remember that whether your swing is hard or soft, the key to a good method is that the clubhead always *accelerates* beneath the ball. Keep your grip pressure light and feel your hands come 'alive' as you thump the sand.

THINK, LISTEN, AND LEARN

The distinctive sounds of golf play a big part in my approach to the game. Particularly around the green, where so much depends on feel and awareness, I associate certain sounds with certain shots. It adds to my sense of control.

When you next go out to practise, try an experiment. Spend the first two or three minutes of your session swinging with your right hand only. Forget about a ball, and focus instead on thumping the heavy flange through the sand. Swivel the clubface open and listen to the sound you make. When you release your right hand correctly the clubhead cuts through the sand with some gusto. It won't take you long to recognize the thrust of a good shot. Work in different areas of the bunker. On the upslope the clubface will tend to dig more deeply than it will on the flat, so get accustomed to that. The downslope is a very different proposition; this time you must encourage the clubface to dig. Instinctively you will learn to swing in sympathy *with* the slope.

That's the real beauty of this exercise. No matter where you are in the sand, if you can make the sound of a good shot you will develop a good technique without even thinking about it.

SENSORY PERCEPTION – THE BEAUTY OF SWINGING WITH YOUR RIGHT HAND ONLY IS THAT YOU DEVELOP A GOOD TECHNIQUE AND CLUBHEAD AWARENESS WITHOUT EVEN THINKING ABOUT IT.

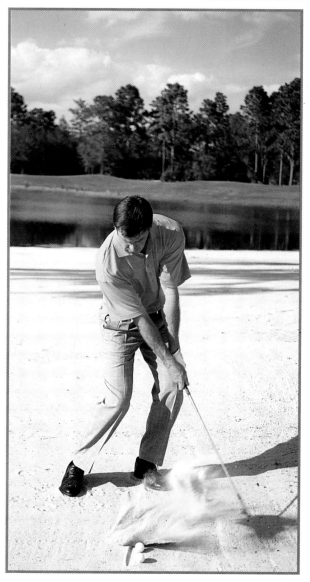

Let's take things a stage further. To have absolute control in the sand you need to get a feel for the bottom of your swing arc. The drill illustrated above will help you to develop that awareness. Set up as if you were about to play a regular splash shot, then draw a line in the sand to bisect your stance. Regard that as your target. Now make a few practice swings and try to cut out a shallow divot of sand, each time thumping the back edge of the clubface on top of that line.

How did you score?

When you can do this with a fair degree of accuracy, place a row of balls a couple of inches forward of the line and play each one in turn. Again, focus on thumping the line, and cut out that shallow divot of sand. You don't have to worry about the ball – as long as you keep to your half of the bargain it will float out every time. With that athletic flexing in your knees maintained for a good balance, vary the length and speed of your swing to regulate distance. Get yourself a rhythm that not only feels good, but *sounds* good.

THE SPIN SHOT – *open the face, zip the ball*

TO ACCENTUATE THE
OPEN CLUBFACE, I
OFTEN THINK IN
TERMS OF 'CUPPING'
MY LEFT WRIST IN THE
BACKSWING, AND
THEN MAINTAINING
THAT ANGLE ALL THE
WAY THROUGH
IMPACT.

Now you have the confidence to thump the sand and trust the clubface, let's see what sort of magic we can conjure up. One of the most desirable trap shots is the spinner that stops on a button – the perfect escape when the pin is just a few feet away. Again, your set up holds the key.

To play this shot I open my stance slightly more than I would to play the regular splash shot, say 40 degrees open to the target, and I also spread my feet a little further apart. These adjustments keep my lower body passive, and also encourage me to hold my hands fractionally lower than normal. You want to be physically 'close' to this shot, ready to cut across the ball with a fairly pronounced wrist action.

One last trick. Choking down on the shaft, make a slight adjustment to your grip. With the clubface already open, turn your left hand to the right of its normal position, and your right hand a little to the left. In other words, *strengthen* the position of your left hand and *weaken* your right. That subtle tweak encourages your hands to open the clubface further during the swing and, more importantly, to keep it open through impact.

Once you are correctly set up, your thoughts should be focused on making the U-shaped swing that enables you to flip the open face beneath the ball. Again, if you simply take your orders from the line of your body, your swing will naturally cut across the ball-to-target line. Here's something to try. In the backswing, rotate your left wrist, so that the club points up towards the sky. In so doing you will find that you open up the clubface to such an extent that no matter how hard you thump the sand, the momentum throws the ball upwards, rather than forwards.

See how short you can hit it with a full swing. In powdery sand I can zip the clubface under the ball at terrific speed and only have it travel a matter of yards. It's up to you to figure out what's possible. Vary the distance you fly the ball with the speed of your swing, and also by gripping down the shaft. I've seen Seve Ballesteros play these shots gripping so far down the shaft his right hand touches the metal. So goes the imagination of a great champion.

A CASE OF 'THUMP
AND TRUST' – A FAIRLY
NORMAL UP AND
DOWN SWING WITH
YOUR 9-IRON
PRODUCES A SHOT
THAT COMES OUT LOW
AND RUNS WILLINGLY
AT THE HOLE.

RUN THE BALL WITH YOUR 9-IRON

If I have a lot of green to work with, anything between 20 and 40 yards to the pin – and this applies particularly when there's a plateau to negotiate – I'll often leave the sand iron in the bag and visualize instead a running shot with a 9-iron. I work on lofting the ball just a few yards out of the bunker, safe in the knowledge that a less lofted club encourages the ball to 'release' with overspin and so run at the hole. It's another string to your bow.

I set up in much the same way that I would to play a regular splash shot, with my body open to the target line and the clubface aimed at the flag. I choke well down on the grip to compensate for the longer shaft of the 9-iron, and play the ball off my left instep. The one noticeable difference is that this time I settle the majority of my weight on my left side. That helps me to create the slightly steeper V-shaped swing necessary to thump the sand and pop the ball out.

When you try this, keep in mind that with its relatively narrow sole, your 9-iron does not have the same degree of bounce that you enjoy with your sand iron, so you really do need to be positive with your swing. I think in terms of sticking the clubhead in the sand about an inch behind the ball, and hitting it hard. The harder you thump the sand, the more the ball will run.

DRILL

Keep your weight left, and thump the sand

In the Short Game chapter I suggested lifting your right heel off the ground to get the feeling of striking *down and through* the shot, and the same drill can help you here. I regularly do this when I practise, hitting balls to flags in that 20 to 40 yard range with my 9-iron. As long as you keep your weight left and accelerate the clubhead to impact, the ball will pop up in a cloud of sand, and run.

I've seen the great Japanese wizard Isao Aoki play these awkward length shots with a 7- or 8-iron. He chokes down on the grip, sticks the clubhead in the sand, and watches as the ball does all the running. Aoki's style is proof, if any were needed, that there are no set rules in the short games. Feel and imagination will always win the day.

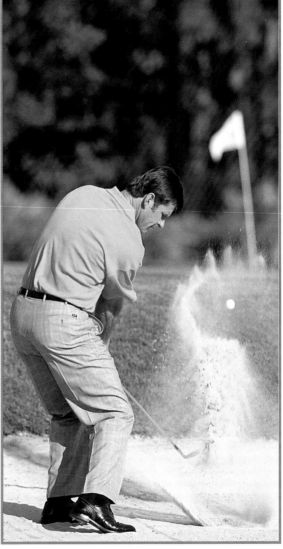

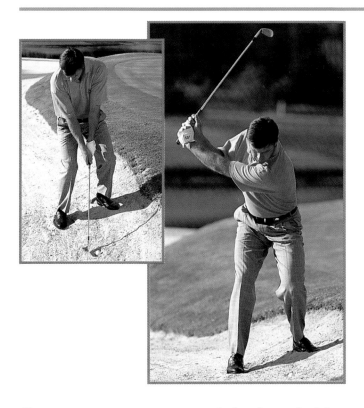

PLUGGED BALL – *Stick the clubhead in the sand*

There's nothing worse than misjudging your approach shot to a green and finding your ball plugged in its own pitch mark. But don't think that you have to create a sand storm to get the ball out. There's a more subtle and effective way. The angle of the clubface is the key. When your ball is partially submerged you need to encourage the clubface to dig in order to remove the necessary divot of sand. To do that you square up the leading edge, thus diminishing the bounce effect. As a general rule, the worse the lie, the more you should close the clubface.

Let's assume the ball is semi-plugged in soft sand. To play this shot I would take a fairly open stance, move the ball back of centre and settle most of my weight on the left side. I then open the clubface just a fraction, and focus on making a fairly steep V-shaped swing with a noticeable wrist break. Aiming to strike a couple of inches behind the ball, I thump the sand with my right hand and leave the clubhead in there. If you set aside some time to practise these shots I think you might be surprised at just how much control you can exert over the ball. It all hinges on feel. The further you want the ball to run, the more you square the face and the harder you thump the sand.

In the extreme case of a fully plugged ball it's worth experimenting with a slightly closed clubface, and you should also consider the option of taking a wedge, as opposed to the sand iron. In other words, eliminate the bounce factor altogether, and concentrate on digging *beneath* the ball. Trust the physics involved. As long as the clubhead is going down, the ball will pop up and out of the bunker. It's impossible to get any backspin, so make sure you allow for a significant amount of run when you visualize the shot.

WHEN THE BALL IS PLUGGED, SQUARE THE FACE AND MAKE YOUR ESCAPE WITH A CONTROLLED THUMP. STICK THE CLUBHEAD IN THE SAND, AND LEAVE IT THERE.

'CHASE' THE CLUBHEAD DOWN THE SLOPE

The way bunkers are designed you can, for the most part, expect to find your ball sitting on the level. But golf wouldn't be half the game it is if your versatility were not always being challenged.

The downhill lie is possibly the most difficult of all sand shots around the green. Resigned to the fact that the ball will come out low with little or no backspin, your thoughts must be geared towards releasing the clubhead down and along the contour of the slope – 'chasing' the ball towards the target. Again, the set-up is fundamental.

Any time your ball comes to rest in such an awkward spot as this, your reaction must be to *neutralize* the effects of the slope. Faced with a downhill lie, lean your spine in sympathy with it, so that you support the majority of your weight on your lower foot. Try to get your hips and shoulders parallel with the run of the ground – or at least as close to parallel as you are comfortably able – then flex your knees for balance.

I would again choke down on the grip, but open the clubface only slightly. Much will depend on the quality of the sand, but generally speaking you don't want too much bounce. If you lay the clubface wide open you are likely to catch the ball with the leading edge and hit the shot 'thin'.

Once you are settled, check the feasibility of making a regular backswing. Playing the ball back in your stance, hinge up your wrists and follow the path of the clubhead. The chances are you will need a fairly pronounced wrist action to avoid touching the sand. To be safe, rehearse your takeaway two or three times and get a feel for the shape of your backswing. To play the shot for real, make your backswing as you planned, then let your hands and arms trace the contours of the slope in the downswing. Visualize the clubface *chasing* the sand beneath the ball and try to keep your head still as you release your right hand. I'm not going to pretend this is easy, because it isn't. But if you base your technique on

this principle of neutralizing the slope with your set-up position, and then commit yourself to releasing the clubhead down and through the sand, you can feel pretty confident of escaping unscathed.

BE AGGRESSIVE ON THE UPSLOPE

The uphill lie is a much easier proposition. This time you lean back until you are able to make a fairly level swing *up the slope*. Your right thigh absorbs the majority of your weight, and your knees work like finely tuned shock absorbers. Shuffle your feet into the sand to establish a firm foundation. Your body must feel anchored and balanced.

As you visualize the shot, keep in mind that even the slightest of upslopes *adds* loft. Each case must be judged on its merits, naturally, but as a general rule you don't need to open the clubface. Aim the leading edge squarely behind the ball, choke down on the shaft and make your regular grip, then commit yourself to being aggressive. Concentrate on making a wide and smooth backswing – there's no need to pick the club up quickly here – and try to hit the sand as tight behind the ball as you can without thinning the shot. The momentum is *upwards* rather than forwards, so don't be afraid to swing hard up the slope.

Faced with a particularly steep uphill lie I will sometimes think in terms of collapsing my left arm as I release the clubhead so that I pull it *up and through* the sand. In other words I thump the sand and then haul the clubface up the slope. In the through-swing my hands work around towards my left shoulder, and in so doing help the ball out. Just another idea you might try.

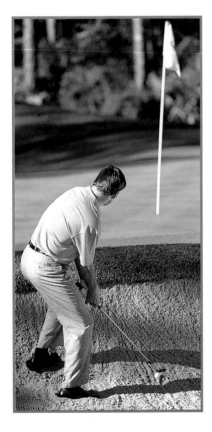

DRILL

'Read' sand and gauge reaction

The process of sizing up any bunker shot begins the moment you step onto the sand. Through your feet you will be able to determine the quality of the surface, and so calculate what you have to work with. Reading sand is an art you develop with experience, but a few general guidelines will set you on your way.

First, be aware that in soft powdery sand the clubhead will naturally want to dig quite deeply. To guard against that, you must adjust your set-up position to create a shallow U-shaped swing. Instinctively you must learn to spread your weight evenly between your feet, and lay the clubface wide open to maximize the bounce effect.

By contrast, on firm sand, or on wet sand compacted by rain, it's your job to make the clubhead dig beneath the ball. Your set-up position this time must be designed to produce a much sharper V-shaped swing. Settle the majority of your weight on your left side and play these shots with a square clubface.

Tied to the quality of the sand, the way your ball is lying in the bunker is another key factor in determining what you can realistically hope to achieve. The depth of sand you have to take to get the clubface fully beneath the ball decides the amount of spin you are able to create. Different lies yield different reactions.

Through the pages of a book no one could teach you how hard to hit a particular shot from a particular lie. This is where your feel for the sand has to take over. What I can do is suggest a drill that I picked up from Gary Player, a simple exercise that quickly teaches you how to gauge sand and judge reaction. It works like this. Arrange four balls in a line, each time making a slightly worse lie: from a perfectly clean lie to a fully plugged ball. Then put the same easy swing on each shot and study the way the ball reacts when it hits the green.

First, the clean lie. No problems here – you can play a normal splash shot with an open clubface and flight the ball with backspin. It may run only 5 or 6 feet on the green so you can afford to be fairly bold. With the ball pressed down only slightly, I would again open the clubface and expect the same swing to produce a marginally lower flight and perhaps 8 or 10 feet of run. The third ball, which is now semi-plugged, will fly lower and run further still, while the fully plugged ball runs most of all.

Go out and see what you can do.

GAMES YOU SHOULD PLAY – SET OUT A LINE OF FOUR BALLS IN A PROGRESSIVELY WORSE LIE, AND GET A FEEL FOR WHAT YOU CAN EXPECT TO ACHIEVE OUT OF THE SAND.

INTERMEDIATE SHOTS – *how to regulate distance*

Sand shots get tougher and tougher the further you are from the green. Those from intermediate range – which I define as being between 30 and 60 yards from the pin – are perhaps the toughest of all.

I work on the theory that you should take a consistent cut of sand – this time aiming about an inch behind the ball – and regulate distance with the length of your swing and subsequent acceleration through impact. I set up in much the same way as I would to play a pitch off the fairway, with my body slightly open to the target and my weight evenly spread between my feet. The one difference is that the ball is back of centre in my stance, and the clubface is now square.

Choking down on the grip of my sand iron, my thoughts are again based on the faithful *rotate and set* philosophy which helps me to produce a relatively shallow downswing. Aiming to make contact with the sand about an inch behind the ball, I make a controlled full backswing, and feel the distance with my acceleration through impact. For me, a shot of 60 yards off good sand would require a fairly upbeat swing and feature a full finish. A slower swing and a balanced three-quarter finish might reflect a shot of 40 yards. You must establish your own range.

BUNKER SHOTS OF BETWEEN 30 AND 60 YARDS DEMAND PRECISION. AIM TO STRIKE THE SAND ABOUT AN INCH BEHIND THE BALL, AND REGULATE DISTANCE WITH THE LENGTH AND SPEED OF YOUR SWING.

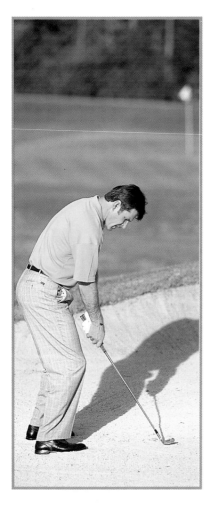

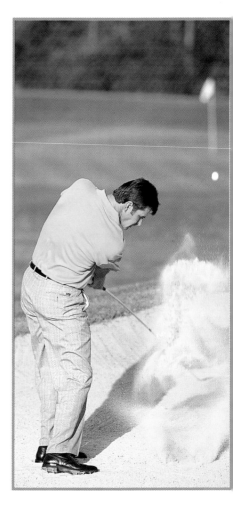

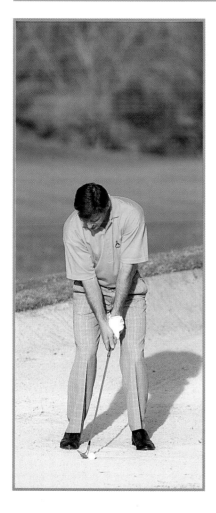

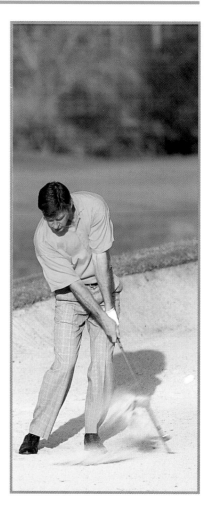

It hardly needs to be said that a good rhythm is fundamental to the outcome. Above all, try to keep your eyes fixed on your target – ie. on the sand an inch or so behind the ball – and your body *centred*. Think of your knees as the shock absorbers that keep you balanced as you turn your trunk back and through. On a delicate footing, the key is to keep your lower body relatively passive, and let your arms and shoulders do the work.

As you get further away from the green, so your strategy will change. There comes a time when you stop aiming to strike the sand first and instead aim to take the ball cleanly. For me that is at around the 60- or 70-yard mark, my limit with the sand iron. I move the ball further back in my stance – to a position opposite my right instep – and focus on clipping the ball as cleanly as possible with a swing built on rhythm and balance.

On a specific point, I find that strengthening my left hand grip helps me guard against picking the club up too steeply in the backswing, which is always a danger when you play the ball back in your stance. Turning your left hand slightly to the right of the normal position encourages you to rotate your left arm correctly away from the ball, and sets you up for a good angle of attack in the downswing.

OVER 60 OR 70 YARDS, YOUR STRATEGY MUST CHANGE. MOVE THE BALL BACK IN YOUR STANCE AND AIM TO CATCH IT 'CLEAN' WITH A FULL SWING.

FAIRWAY BUNKER SHOTS – *club up and swing easy*

On any fairway bunker shot my initial thought pattern runs like this: what sort of lie do I have to play with, and how severe is the front lip of the bunker? Taken together – and usually in that order – these factors determine what is possible and what is not. My advice is, be rational not reckless. Without a club, step into the bunker, find out how the ball is lying and feel the texture of the sand through your feet. If the possibility of playing a full shot at the green exists, how far do you have to fly the ball? Will the club that you need to cover that distance give you the trajectory to clear the front lip? These are the questions that need answers.

If the lie is poor, your decision is as good as made for you. Play safe. Where would you most like to be playing your *next* shot from? Determine a safety zone, and then plot the easiest route back to the fairway. Don't bite off more than you can chew; it's all too easy to waste shots, and much, much harder to get them back.

Let's look on the brighter side. Conditions are favourable. You have a shot of some 140 yards to the green, a good lie, and the front lip of the bunker is fairly negligible. My immediate reaction in this sort of situation is always to club up. Off the fairway, a shot of this distance would normally call for an 8-iron, but I would opt for the 7 in the bunker. With that little extra power I know I can swing comfortably *within myself* and still achieve the required distance.

The details are relatively unchanged. I play the ball in the middle of my stance, settle my weight pretty much evenly between my feet and choke down on the grip. All I'm interested in now is making a silky-smooth swing and picking the ball cleanly off the sand. As soon as you force a shot like this you are liable to lose your footing and your strike is in jeopardy.

Whether or not this is peculiar to me I don't know, but I find that moving my body ever so slightly towards the target in the downswing helps me keep my hands ahead of the clubface and meet the ball cleanly (remember, thin is better than fat). With what amounts to a slight sway, I *ease* myself into the shot. My eyes are fixed on the back of the ball, and I tell myself to 'stay tall and watch it' as I make my downswing. I keep my footwork to a minimum, and accelerate the clubhead all the way to a full and balanced finish.

WINDING AND UNWINDING YOUR UPPER BODY OVER A QUIET LEG ACTION IS THE ESSENCE OF A GOOD SWING, AND THE KEY TO STRIKING THE BALL CLEANLY.

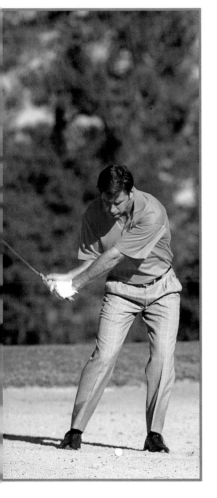

10

PLAYING
THE GAME

*When I retire from the tournament circuit, I want to be able
to look back on my career satisfied that I gave 100 per cent –
not just to the act of striking the golf ball, but mentally playing the game.*

If you could join me on the practice tee at any professional tournament around the world, you would experience at first hand the tremendous talent that exists in golf today. From the fairways of the Far East, to the US Tour, and at home in Europe, such is the quality of the competition that only the strongest and most determined can hope to survive.

Take the issue of ball-striking, relative to scoring. I see many young players who are highly impressive on the range, where there is no pressure on their swing, nothing riding on their performance. Out on the course, theory becomes reality. Now the *competitive instinct* is challenged. Every time you set foot on the tee, you are entering the unknown, which is why skills of self-control and mental toughness largely determine your success. The professionals who consistently make the grade are the players who can take in their stride all the unpredictable bounces and different lies that make up a typical round of golf. It's the same at club level. There is always someone who stands out, a player who has that something extra, be it the *feel* in his hands, or a stomach for pressure. Or simply the guts to make something happen.

You only get out of this game what you are prepared to put in to it. That philosophy is true to life, and I firmly believe in it. Whatever your personal goals may be, to win the club championship, shoot your first score under 100, or break that magical figure of 70, you need determination to make the breakthrough. If you are willing to work at your game, and discover all the variables that make it such a great voyage of discovery . . . who knows? Here are a few ideas to ponder.

MIND GAMES – PRETEND YOU HAVE TO FLIGHT A GENTLE FADE WITH A 5-IRON TO THE FINAL FLAG. GO TO THE PRACTICE GREEN AND IMAGINE YOU HAVE 'THIS 5-FOOTER' FOR THE OPEN CHAMPIONSHIP.

HOW TO PRACTISE FOR REAL

I'll be the first to endorse the value of hitting balls on the practice tee to groove a sound technique. There is no substitute for repetition, but don't be blinkered in your approach. With a little imagination you can embrace the real challenge of the game.

Here's a trick I use from time to time to improve both my powers of visualization *and* my resilience to pressure. Say I'm practising for the Masters at Augusta. Having warmed up for a few minutes, my thoughts turn to my game plan. I imagine that I'm standing on the first tee, and try to picture the shape of the hole in my mind. I then take the appropriate club, at Augusta that's usually a driver, and go ahead and hit my opening drive. Now the ball is in play and, watching its flight, I can pretty much determine where I would have finished on the hole. Scanning the course planner, my caddy figures out the yardage to the green. I then apply the same set of rules to my second shot, and so it goes on. You can take this 'virtual reality' to the limits. If I hit a bad one, and I'm standing near a piece of rough, I will often drop a ball down in the rough and play the shot as I would expect to find it on the course. All the time, my mind is *seeing* the relevant picture and telling my body what to do. And that's the trick to making your practice session more productive.

Conditioning your mental state in this fashion can also help you overcome bouts of anxiety, or nervousness on the course. If you rehearse this visualization technique in practice, you will get some idea of how your swing holds up under pressure. Challenge yourself to shape the ball to suit the shape of that hole, just as you hope to do for real out on the course. If you fear a 'bogey' hole, play it over and over again in your mind, until your anxiety ebbs away.

There is a great deal written about the mental side of this game that makes good sense. But, equally, there is a tendency to make too much of what is essentially a simple matter. This is how I sum up my 'inner' philosophy: *If you are nervous about hitting your driver straight down the fairway, you need to go away and hit balls until you feel more confident.* Similarly, if you dread facing a short putt on the final green, set aside some time to practise your putting until you overcome your fear. Practise hard enough, and you can actually reach the stage where you look forward to holing a putt for the match.

TAKE A HALF SET, TEST YOUR IMAGINATION

Here's another idea to spice up your practice time.

The day after the Open at Muirfield in 1992, I played a friendly game at Swinley Forest, a wonderful tree-lined course in Berkshire. The old caddie who greeted me at the clubhouse was lost for words when I handed him a small lightweight bag, which contained just a half-set of clubs – driver, 2-iron, 5-iron, 8-iron, wedge and putter. I thoroughly enjoyed my round, and shot 65.

To anyone who plays the game, strolling a course with just a handful of clubs could be the most enjoyable and worthwhile practice time you can have. I could play on my own for hours . . . a challenge match, two balls against each other, odd number versus even. Or draw against fade. What better way to test the quality of your shot-making and sharpen your imagination?

Play in the early morning or late in the evening, when the course is quiet. Alone with your thoughts, you can nominate a cut-up shot one minute, then punch the ball the next. Bend shots around trees; make the ball turn both ways.

Perhaps more than anything else, playing with just a few clubs teaches you the art of manufacturing speciality shots and judging distance. Where you might normally expect to play a 6-iron, but don't have one, you are forced to nudge a quiet 5. Or hit a hard 7. The trick is to visualize the shot, pick out your landing area, and give yourself just one go at it. That's the key to staying competitive – both mentally and physically.

'Target' your game, Sharpen your focus

Playing a few holes on your own will also give you the opportunity to try this simple experiment. On a typical par-4, tee-up a ball as close as you can to the left-hand marker. Set up to the ball and take a look down the fairway. Then tee another as close as possible to the right hand marker, and compare the view.

 If you play with a natural fade as I do, you will feel more comfortable playing from the right-hand corner of the tee. That suits your shape, and offers you the most inviting view of the fairway. It *maximizes* your target area. If you draw the ball, the left side of the tee is where you will feel most comfortable. And remember, there is nothing in the rules to prevent your standing *outside* the teeing area, as long as your ball is teed-up between the markers.

TUNNEL VISION – WHETHER ON THE TEE OR ON THE FAIRWAY, PICK OUT A SPECIFIC TARGET AND SEE THE SHOT BEFORE YOU HIT IT.

Here's something else to consider. The rules allow you to tee your ball up to a maximum of two club lengths *behind* the tee-blocks. That gives you some leeway to play with, which can be useful when you get an 'in-between' yardage on a par-3. Let's assume a hole measures 160 yards. For me, a good 6-iron flies around 165-yards, and in this example, the pin is out of the range with a 7. The solution? If I tee the ball back by the two yards I am allowed, that will often make the difference between hitting 'easy' and hitting full.

One more word of advice. I rarely play a ball 'off the deck', or knock up a piece of turf as a makeshift tee. This is the one time you have the opportunity to give yourself a perfectly clean lie, so make the most of it.

Playing a new venue each week tends to keep my mind relatively fresh to the challenge of plotting a realistic course from tee to green. I know how far I hit the ball and, like most professionals, I play the 'yardage game'. The process of *targeting* my shots clearly in my mind has become an integral part of my preshot routine, and it should be a part of yours. One or two simple rules can save you valuable shots.

First, don't stand on the tee and regard the entire width of the fairway as your target area. Not only is that much too vague, it opens the door for complacency. Unless you have a specific target against which to measure your performance off the tee, you can never hope to be consistent.

The key is to *sharpen* your focus with 'tunnel vision'. Allowing for your natural shape, take dead aim on some specific object – perhaps a tree, or a distant rooftop – anything that enables you to pinpoint your alignment. Give yourself a margin for error. With a driver, I usually stand behind the ball and picture in my mind's eye a circle in the fairway, say 10 yards across. That's a comfortable and realistic safety zone.

While you at least have the benefit of a flag to identify your ultimate target, you must also discipline your approach play. All the time you are walking up to your ball, you should be forming a picture in your mind of the shot you have to play. Then, once on the scene, stand behind the ball and 'go to the movies'. 'See' the shot unfold before you step up to play it. Make a note of any trouble that exists around the green, exact yardages, pin placement, and so on.

Know your limitations and exercise restraint when necessary. Don't shoot for the pin if it is cut tight to the edge, with a deep bunker lurking nearby. Play on the safe side; go for the heart of the green, and take your chances with the putter.

On a specific note, think about the pin position in relation to the *depth* of the green when you survey your yardage. Most amateurs I play with tend to come up short of the hole more often than not. The point to remember is this: if a green measures 40 paces from front to back, you could be hitting anything from a 7-iron to a 4-iron, depending on where the pin is placed. Use your yardage book diligently.

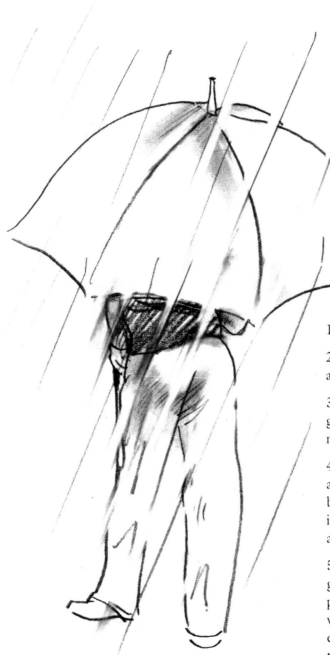

COME RAIN OR SHINE

Members at Welwyn Garden City used to think me mad when I would stand alone on the practice ground hitting balls in wind and rain. But you have to be prepared for any and every eventuality, and that includes swinging the club with a set of waterproofs on.

Think about what you must do to give yourself the best possible chance of hitting a good shot. *Club up, swing easy* – that's one of my wet-weather rules. Remember, the ball isn't going to run very far; you have to carry it all the way. As a further precaution, I would also grip down the shaft a little. That helps me protect against catching the ground fat. In 'heavy' conditions, you're much better off taking the ball cleanly off the turf.

Some common-sense ideas on playing wet-weather golf:

1. Pack at least *two* dry towels in your bag.

2. If you wear a glove, carry two or three spares, preferably in a polythene bag.

3. Make sure that any waterproof clothing you buy is generous in fitting, and does not restrict your movement in any way.

4. Be extra careful around the green. Surface water can accumulate very quickly, so check your route to the hole before playing any sort of running shot. Where ordinarily you might choose to chip the ball, you may find the aerial route is your most viable option.

5. Sand play – square up the clubface. When you face a greenside bunker shot, and the sand is wet and compacted, your sand iron will not 'bounce' as willingly as it would do normally. You must encourage the leading edge to dig, so set up this shot with the clubface relatively square. In severe conditions, use your pitching wedge.

6. Putting – play for less break. On a wet surface, the ball will not take the borrow as readily as it does on dry, quick greens.

CUT YOUR LOSSES, GET BACK IN PLAY

One of the keys to consistent scoring is what I call 'damage limitation'. When I get into trouble, I think in terms of getting safely back into play. There's a simple procedure you need to follow: ask yourself what you stand to gain, and compare that with what you stand to lose. If you apply that line of thinking, the solution should make itself very clear. Your first consideration must always be the quality of your lie. If the ball is lying cleanly, and you can get a swing at it, then by all means entertain thoughts of a good recovery. But realize your personal limitations. I would suggest you adhere to what I call my '90 per cent rule'. If I think I have at least a 90 per cent chance of pulling off a fancy shot, then I take it. Otherwise I take the conservative route, and play for the fairway. I think a couple of moves ahead, and determine exactly from where I would like to be playing my *next* shot.

Long grass presents you with a further problem. Any time your ball ends up in the rough, the danger is that the grass wraps itself around the hosel – the angle between the clubface and shaft – and turns the toe of the clubface over, causing you to pull the shot left. You run the risk of smothering the ball. One way to guard against this happening is to grip the club a little more firmly than normal with your left hand, and open the face a touch at address. Then make a relatively steep up-and-down swing, and thump the back of the ball.

Beware of the 'flier', also. In light rough, and you are particularly vulnerable when the grass is wet, a well-struck shot will often fly 10 or 20 yards farther than normal. Blades of grass get trapped between the clubface and the ball, and so little or no spin is imparted. Club yourself accordingly.

WHEN THE BALL IS ABOVE YOUR FEET . . .

The only place you can expect to find a perfectly level lie is on the tee. After that it's a lottery. You can hit a great drive down the middle of the fairway only to find your ball resting in a divot. On another hole you find an awkward lie with the ball above the level of your feet. Or below the level of your feet. So you need to be versatile.

As a rule of thumb, I choke down on the grip just a little any time I find my ball 'off the level'. That enhances my feel and sense of control. Then I make the necessary adjustments in my stance to maintain a good balance in the swing. That's the key. If the ball is above the level of your feet, then naturally you will need to stand a little more erect than normal. Settle your weight evenly between your feet, and position the ball opposite the middle of your stance.

Accept the fact that your swing is destined to be fairly flat and rounded, causing the ball to spin from right to left through the air. Take that into account when you visualize the shot. Aim both your body and the clubface to the *right* of your intended target, then focus on swinging the club with balance and rhythm.

Now for a trick the more experienced player might try. If ever I need to *neutralize* the slope (that is, to impart a counter-spin in order to keep the ball flying relatively straight), I focus on trying to keep the heel of the club moving faster than the toe through impact. That's my swing thought. In other words, I try to *hold off* the release, with the hint of a cutting action, keeping my left hand and left forearm firm through the ball. Try this in practice before you try it for real.

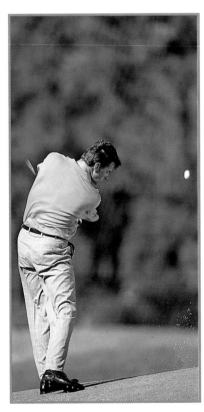

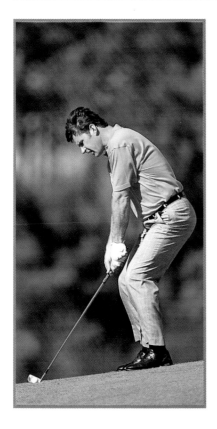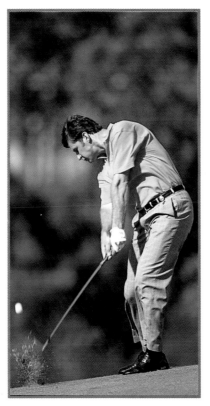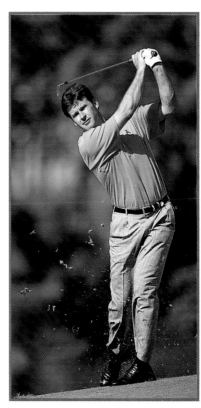

. . . AND BELOW YOUR FEET

Throughout this book I have stressed the role of the knees in the golf swing, and here is no exception. Any time the ball is below your feet, and this is generally regarded as the tougher of the two shots, your knees hold the answer. As you set up to the ball, use them as shock absorbers, and build a stable stance and posture that enables you to rotate your upper body in balance.

Spread your feet a little wider than normal, then flex your knees until your spine is set at a relatively normal angle. As you lean forward stick out your rear and feel your weight is supported on the balls of your feet.

This time you can expect your swing to be a little more upright than normal, causing the ball to fly with left-to-right spin. Adjust your aim accordingly, and try to make a fairly relaxed, smooth swing. The left-to-right shape will cost you distance, so club up and swing easy.

Anyone with ambition should again experiment, and learn how to manufacture a straight shot from a 'hanging' lie. In this case, with the ball below my feet, I would focus on turning the toe *over* the heel through impact, just as if I were trying to play a draw. With practice, you can learn to feel these shots in your hands and arms, and so neutralize the effect of the slope.

UPHILL AND DOWNHILL

When your ball comes to rest on an upslope, it will naturally tend to fly higher than normal. The angle of the slope effectively *adds* loft to the clubface, so as a general rule you need to take at least one club more than the distance would ordinarily dictate. On the downslope, the opposite is true. When your swing follows a downhill slope, the clubface is effectively *delofted* at impact, and the ball flies with a lower trajectory than normal. Accordingly, take less club.

There are two ways to go about playing these shots. Let's deal with the up-slope first. On a gentle incline, I would suggest that you first try to compensate for the effect of the slope by tilting your body to the right until your spine was more or less *perpendicular* with the ground. In other words, try to set up as normal, but at a slight angle, with the majority of your weight naturally settled on your back foot.

Once you have established good balance, you can make a relatively normal swing, and your arc will follow the slope through impact. Swing easy, and take at least one extra club to compensate for the higher flight.

On a more severe slope, the problem you face is one of keeping the ball *down*. If you lean back in sympathy with the slope, it's very difficult to drive the ball forward. As an alternative strategy, I tend to lean gently *against* the slope, keeping my right leg relatively straight, and flex my left knee for balance. Taking at least one, and possibly two clubs more than the distance would normally require, I then aim to strike down with a controlled, three-quarter punching action.

The key to this shot is the shape of the follow-through. See how my left arm folds away very early after impact: remember this is a controlled, three-quarter punch. The feeling I have is that of striking the ball against the slope, and then pulling the clubface up the hill, so that the divot taken is minimal.

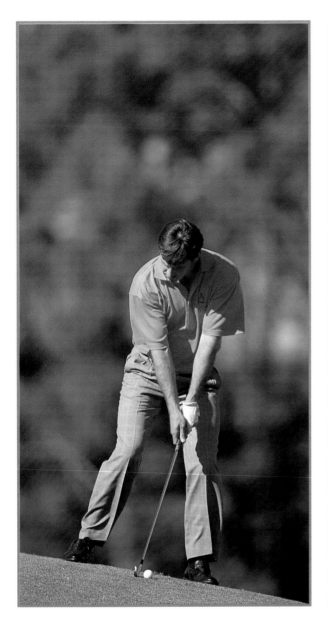

The downslope could be the hardest of all these so-called 'problem' lies. This time you have only one option: you must set up to the ball in sympathy with the slope, with your spine perpendicular to the ground, and the majority of your weight on your lower foot. Rehearse your set-up and make a practice swing to the side of the ball. Stand there and take a divot. That tells you where the club meets the ground, so when you set up to the shot for real, your ball position is taken care of.

The tough thing in this instance is getting the ball airborne. As the club is *delofted*, the ball will tend to fly relatively low, with little or no backspin. So

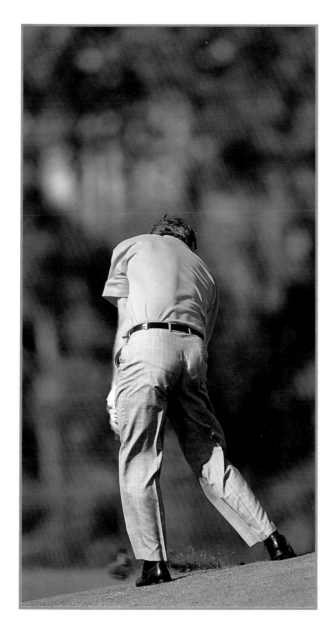 

think hard about where you should land the ball, and visualize the shot running much of the way to your target. Any time I face a shot off a severe downhill lie, I will often concentrate on picking the club up quite steeply in the backswing, and play a cut-up type shot. That makes it easier to get the clubface fully under the ball, though you do need to allow for the shot to fade quite dramatically. Another good swing thought is to 'chase' the clubhead down the contours of the slope through and beyond impact. Commit yourself to releasing the club fully, and stay *down* on the shot.

LONG IRONS – *think 'scrape it and sweep it'*

Long irons are difficult to get into the air. I can remember having trouble as a youngster, but the problem is often more psychological than physical. One of the best tips I was ever given to ease the problem was this: when you move the club away, make sure that you *scrape* the grass behind the ball then, on the way through, aim to clip the grass beyond the ball as you *sweep* it away. Say the words out loud when you practise: 'scrape the grass, and sweep the ball'.

With the longer clubs particularly, your finish is all important. Practise walking

through the shot to get used to the sensation of finishing your swing with your weight on your left side, and with your right shoulder the closest part of your body to the target. Try to make yourself release the clubhead and wrap the shaft around your neck. Remember, it's always better to move forward through the ball – watch Gary Player go after his longer shots. Fall backwards, and you're more likely to top the shot, or worse, hit it fat. Don't ever imagine that you need to swing your longer clubs any harder than you do your short irons. Far better to make yourself swing a little slower. That way you give your body sufficient time to wind and unwind correctly.

'SCALP' THE BALL OFF A BARE LIE

The key to playing any shot off a bare lie is setting up in such a way that the leading edge of the club can make clean contact with the bottom of the ball. Here's a tough proposition. Imagine you have 30 yards to the pin, the ball is lying on hard, bare ground, and there's a bunker between you and the hole. In this case, when you need to be certain of applying loft, make sure that you set up with the clubface *square*. That way you eliminate any tendency for the club-head to 'bounce' through impact. To encourage a good angle of attack, play the ball back of centre in your stance.

The one thing you must not do is tense up. So many amateur golfers tighten their grip on the club whenever they feel threatened, and that just kills any hope they have of making a smooth swing. If anything, I actually *lighten* my grip pressure to play these shots. That helps me to relax my wrists, so they hinge freely back and through the shot.

Ultimately, it all boils down to practice. Keep your head and body dead still, and trust the loft on the clubface to do its job as you 'scalp' the ball cleanly. As your confidence grows you will find that you are able to judge distance fairly accurately, cut things pretty fine and get close to the hole.

STAY IN THE 'HERE AND NOW'

Thinking too far ahead is a common mistake in golf.
I'm guilty of it myself from time to time. Sometimes
it's a testimony to the quality of the course you are
playing. Take Augusta National, for example. Often
my mind wanders ahead to the twelfth, long before I
reach that mischievous little hole. The same thing can
happen at Cypress Point, where the par-3 sixteenth,
which features a long carry across the ocean, can
strike into your heart. It's stating the obvious to say a
round of golf comprises 18 holes, and that they are all
important, but if you can learn to play one hole at a
time, you will score better and better. To fulfil
whatever potential you have, you need the mental
resilience to focus on playing one shot, one hole, at a
time.

Every now and then I complete a round and I have
no idea how many shots I've played. That's the
ultimate mental state, and I wish it would happen
more often. But amateurs have usually calculated they
need to finish 4,4,4 for a career best score. They lose
sight of the task at hand and make mistakes. As soon
as you start rehearsing the winner's speech, you're in
trouble. If you really want to win, try to stay in the
here and now. The best players in the world are the
players who have the discipline to hit a shot and
forget it. They make birdies, and bank them.

IF YOU HAVE A BAD
HOLE, PUT IT OUT OF
YOUR MIND. IF I TAKE
A SEVEN, I TRY TO
CONVINCE MYSELF
THAT A WEEK HAS
ELAPSED. FORGET IT.

HOW TO WIN AT MATCHPLAY

'Don't give an inch', that's my philosophy to playing matchplay golf. Make your opponent *win* holes, don't give them away. If a player makes birdies and beats me head to head, then fine, as long as I gave 100 per cent and didn't throw the game away. *Never* give up. Playing in the final of the World Matchplay Championship at Wentworth in 1993 against American Ryder Cup player Corey Pavin, I made a mess of the final hole. Having clawed my way back into the game, I first ballooned my drive at this relatively short par-5, then blocked my 3-wood second shot into the trees, right of the green. Pavin had hit a reasonably good drive, and looked to have the title safely in his pocket. Finding my ball in an unplayable lie, I was forced to take a penalty drop, and took two more shots to reach the green in five. I then made my 20-footer for a bogey six, forcing Pavin to make a very missable 4-footer of his own for a winning par. That's the crux. He had to *win* the tournament – I made him work for it.

Here are one or two random observations.

Keep the pressure on. If you have just won a hole, and the next is a par-3, make sure you find the green. If you miss the target, you can just about guarantee that your opponent will hit it, and the flow of the game changes.

Don't expect to be given 2-footers. Before any serious game, spend a few minutes practising those 2- and 3-footers – build your confidence in this 'gimme' range. I would suggest working hard on your short game, too. There is nothing more likely to upset an opponent than your ability to 'scramble', to repeatedly get 'up and down'.

Don't let a big-hitter upset your normal strategy. Frankly, I'd rather have the pleasure of playing my second shot first, and hopefully put the pressure back on an opponent who is longer off the tee. No matter how far you hit the ball, it's harder to play a good approach shot when your opponent is already sitting pretty on the green, somewhere near the hole.

Don't take unnecessary risks. What constitutes a risk will, to some degree, be determined by the state of your match. If you're four holes down with four to play, then really you have nothing to lose. Gamble as a last resort. If your match is evenly balanced and your opponent drives out of bounds, or finds other trouble, rethink your own strategy. Put your driver back in your bag, and take the conservative route with a 3-wood, or long iron.

LIVE AND LEARN

Making mistakes is a natural part of trying to do better. In golf, mistakes can be humbling, and they can sometimes be expensive. But they should always be valuable. Specific incidents will stick in your mind. I remember a tournament in Italy. All I had to do was get up-and-down with a simple chip shot to stay in touch with the leaders over the closing holes. There was nothing to go over, but I took a wedge, and the ball checked up several feet short of the pin. I missed the putt, and with it my chance was gone. You don't forget moments like that. Now, any time I find myself in a similar situation off the edge of the green, I am inclined to reach for an 8- or 9-iron, just to make sure the ball gets up to the hole. There are many other examples. The point is, every time I make a mistake, I learn a valuable lesson.

Above all else, be honest with yourself. When you make a mistake, own up to the responsibility. Every golfer keeps a mental library of events, as they occur, but it's not a bad idea to sit down quietly after a game and make a note of any significant shots or poor decisions you may have made. Better still, spend a few minutes on the practice tee after your round is over, and address any problem areas while they are still fresh in your mind. That's the professional approach.

I HATE WHEN PEOPLE TELL ME I'VE MADE A MISTAKE, BUT I'M NOT TOO PROUD TO ADMIT MISTAKES TO MYSELF.

TOURNAMENT VICTORIES

1977   Skol Lager Individual
1978   Colgate P.G.A. Championship
1979   ICL Tournament (SA)
1980   Sun Alliance P.G.A. Championship
1981   Sun Alliance P.G.A. Championship
1982   Haig Tournament Players Championship
1983   Pace Rabanne French Open
        Martini International
        Car Care Plan International
        Lawrence Batley
        Ebel Swiss Masters
1984   Heritage Classic (US)
        Car Care Plan International
1987   Peugeot Spanish Open
        Open Championship
1988   French Open
        Volvo Masters
1989   U.S. Masters
        Volvo P.G.A. Championship
        Dunhill British Masters
        French Open
        Suntory World Match Play Championship
1990   U.S. Masters
        Open Championship
        Johnnie Walker Asian Classic
1991   Carrolls Irish Open
1991   Carrolls Irish Open
        Open Championship
        Scandinavian Masters
        European Open
        Toyota World Match Play Championship
        Johnnie Walker World Championship
1993   Johnnie Walker Classic
        Carrolls Irish Open
1994   Alfred Dunhill Open
        Million Dollar Challenge
1995   Doral Ryder Open